Men, Masculinity, and the Indian Act

Men, Masculinity, and the Indian Act

Martin J. Cannon

UBCPress · Vancouver · Toronto

28 27 26 25 24 23 22 21 20   5 4 3 2

Printed in Canada on FSC-certified ancient-forest-free paper (100% post-consumer recycled) that is processed chlorine- and acid-free.

ISBN 978-0-7748-6095-6 (hardcover)
ISBN 978-0-7748-6096-3 (pbk.)
ISBN 978-0-7748-6097-0 (PDF)
ISBN 978-0-7748-6098-7 (EPUB)
ISBN 978-0-7748-6099-4 (Kindle)

Cataloguing-in-publication data for this book is available from Library and Archives Canada.

Canadä

UBC Press gratefully acknowledges the financial support for our publishing program of the Government of Canada (through the Canada Book Fund), the Canada Council for the Arts, and the British Columbia Arts Council.

This book has been published with the help of a grant from the Canadian Federation for the Humanities and Social Sciences, through the Awards to Scholarly Publications Program, using funds provided by the Social Sciences and Humanities Research Council of Canada.

Printed and bound in Canada by Friesens
Set in Univers and Giovanni by Artegraphica Design Co. Ltd.
Substantive editor: Lesley Erickson
Proofreader: Caitlin Gordon-Walker
Indexer: Judy Dunlop
Cover designer: Will Brown

UBC Press
The University of British Columbia
2029 West Mall
Vancouver, BC V6T 1Z2
www.ubcpress.ca

This book is dedicated to the memory of
Gregory G. Cannon, 1962–2013

Contents

Nyawen Skannoh

ACKNOWLEDGMENTS

T HE IDEA FOR THIS book originated in 1988 after reading feminist theory and later, during my graduate research, when I focused on Indigenous women's writings on sexism and racism. I continued to think about these issues at Queen's and York Universities in the 1990s, when I more purposefully started to realize my identity as a Haudenosaunee person and to theorize the combined effects of racism and sexism. I thank classmates and faculty who encouraged me to think about these issues, especially Roberta Hamilton, Mary Morton, and Ena Dua.

I am passionate about this book's content. It represents a culmination of thinking about sexism and its impact on men as Indigenous persons. There are many people I must acknowledge for helping me to realize this book. I especially thank Darcy Cullen of UBC Press and the late Virgil Duff of University of Toronto Press for their generous support and patience. I thank Ann Macklem at UBC Press who helped realize the book's production. I am also very grateful to Angela Pietrobon for her diligent and dedicated editorial assistance at every turn.

A number of colleagues and friends have supported and challenged me over the years. I am grateful to the late Trish

(Patricia) Monture for being a mentor, friend, and colleague during my appointment at the University of Saskatchewan. I would also like to thank other colleagues, including John Borrows, Susan Dion, Jane Griffith, Susan M. Hill, Bev Jacobs, Bonita Lawrence, Darlene Rose Okemaysim-Sicotte, Audra Simpson, Verna St. Denis, and Lina Sunseri. Although I am responsible for the ideas and insights put forward in this book, they have either supported me or shaped my ideas and thinking.

I also acknowledge the graduate students with whom I have worked since my appointment at the Ontario Institute for Studies in Education in 2007. I would like to thank my friends for their love and support over many years, especially Marc Sanderson and the late Michael Monture. I thank my parents and my immediate and extended family for their interest in and support of my work. I also give thanks to all my maternal relations, the Six Nations at Grand River Territory, for ongoing inspiration.

Men, Masculinity, and the Indian Act

Introduction

IN THE MID-TWENTIETH century, Indigenous women in Canada began to speak out against the Indian Act, the principal statute under which Canada administers Indian status. They argued that the Indian Act was sexist, that it created inequality between First Nations women and men. In particular, they opposed section 12(1)(b), which took away Indian status from Indigenous women who married non-Status Indian men, and section 11(1)(f), which conferred status on non-Indigenous or white settler women who married Status Indian men. These sections had formerly been sections 3(c) of the 1876 Indian Act. In the 1970s, women such as Jeannette Corbiere Lavell and Yvonne Bédard, women who had lost their status upon marriage, took their cases all the way to the Supreme Court, and when they lost, women's groups across the country pressured the government to change the law. The government was forced to act when Sandra Lovelace took her case to the United Nations Human Rights Committee, which found Canada in breach of the International Covenant on Civil and Political Rights.

In 1982, Canada amended its Constitution to include the Canadian Charter of Rights and Freedoms, which protects every individual from "discrimination based on race, national or ethnic origin, colour, religion, sex, age, or mental or physical disability." Motivated to address the Indian Act, the government passed Bill C-31, An Act to Amend the Indian Act, in April 1985. Its stated goals were to address the gender discrimination of the Indian Act, to restore Indian status to those who had been involuntarily enfranchised (those who had had their status taken away), and to allow bands to control their own band membership, a step towards self-government. The act terminated sections 12(1)(b) and 11(1)(f), and it restored the status of Indian women who had been enfranchised. It immediately resulted in 127,000 individuals having their status restored, and 106,000 individuals having it taken away (Trovat and Aylsworth 2012). Section 6 of the act, "Persons Entitled to be Registered," introduced two new classes of Indians: "6(1) – those who can pass Indian status to their children" and "6(2) – those who have Indian status, but cannot pass their status to their children unless the other parent also has status" (Mccue 2011).

Although these developments appeared to be progressive, and in many ways were, they ushered in decades of divisive debates in Indigenous communities and internal disputes about identity, authenticity, and belonging. They pitted individual women against Status Indians and women against men. There were exceptions, but Indigenous men and Indigenous organizations did not support these women's attempt to overcome sexism in the Indian Act. They feared that more and more involuntarily enfranchised women would return to reserves along with their husbands, placing pressure on land and resources. In the context of the human rights discourses of the 1970s and 1980s, they also feared they would lose their special-status citizenship rights to education, health, social services, and land, which are protected under the Indian Act. They did not want the Canadian Bill of Rights (which protects individual rights) to assume precedence over the Indian Act (which protects collective rights) and therefore opposed the actions of women such as Lavell and Bédard (Canada 1973; Cannon 1995; Green 1997).[1] As Kathleen Jamieson (1986, 125) wrote at the time, "The acute shortage of adequate housing on most reserves and the intensity of inter-clan political rivalries on many of those same reserves combine[d] to make the issue particularly volatile and the women particularly vulnerable to victimization."

FROM MY PERSPECTIVE, the politics of Indian status in these decades – which revolved around discussions of "women's rights" versus "Aboriginal rights" or "individual" versus "collective" rights – didn't make much sense at all. Nor did the stance of Indigenous men. Today, I am a federally recognized Indian man and a scholar. I am a member of the Onyota'a:ka (Oneida Nation), Turtle Clan, and a citizen of the Six Nations at Grand River Territory. Until 1985, however, as a "mixed-race" male whose mother had married a non-Indian, I was denied recognition under the Indian Act. I was an involuntarily enfranchised male, but debates in academic circles, Indigenous communities, and the courts were not addressing my situation, or that of other men like me (Cannon 2007a, 39). They were focusing instead on how the sexism of the Indian Act was harming women, on how individual women and their cases were threatening Indigenous nations, or on how the rights of women were being sacrificed in favour of the rights of First Nations to engage in self-determination. From my perspective, however, it looked like the sexism in the Indian Act was actually affecting all Indigenous people – women and men – and undermining the collective rights of our nations by taking away our ability to determine who does or doesn't belong.

Under Canada's Indian Act (and the way it is currently understood), my mother and I were forced to bifurcate our identities into impossible either/or categorizations. My mother could either be a Status Indian or a woman but not both. But, as Patricia Monture-Angus, a Mohawk activist, lawyer, and author, has noted (1995, 136–37), it is simply impossible to separate out whether it is sexism or racialized injustice that impacts us as Indigenous men and women:

> My life experiences are as both a Mohawk and a woman. I cannot say when I can name an act as discrimination, that it happened to me because I am a Mohawk or because I am a woman. I cannot take the woman out of the Mohawk or the Mohawk out of the woman. It feels like all one package to me. I exist as a single person. My experience is "discrimination within discrimination" ... It is wound together through my experiences. This is very different from this idea of double discrimination. But the court could not even get to this first step, they could not see that two grounds of discrimination were occurring at the same time. In the court's view, discrimination is competitive. One form of discrimination must triumph.

Similarly, under Canadian law, I was not an "authentic" or "real" Indian (Lawrence 2004) because my father is a *ha dih nyoh* (the word in my language for white settler). Under traditional law, however, it is of no matter that my father is of Anglo-British descent. It matters only that my mother and grandmothers are from the Onyota'a:ka Nation, a matrilineal culture in which women are esteemed. Haudenosaunee (meaning "we build the house together," a reference to the distinctive houses in which my ancestors once resided as Six Nations, including the Seneca, Cayuga, Onondaga, Oneida, Mohawk, and Tuscarora Nations) look to relatives on the female side of the family to understand who we are as nations and peoples. In my nation, a person's clan affiliation is matrilineal – it is determined through one's mother and grandmothers. Our people have been determined to document, remember, and preserve this practice of kinship organization at every turn (North American Indian Travelling College 1984, 1993). It is my responsibility to identify as Haudenosaunee and as Turtle Clan, not as "mixed" or "Métis," and it is my responsibility as a Haudenosaunee man to question and resist discrimination directed at our mothers and grandmothers.[2]

It is nothing short of remarkable that we continue to remember and preserve the robust cultural knowledges of our ancestors where identity and nationhood are concerned. In responding to federally imposed categories of identity and citizenship, some of us look to traditional stories in a way that invariably transforms how we think about ourselves and our dealings with others. Our stories shape the way we think about identity and belonging, and they are especially relevant to how we are decolonizing ourselves and our nations. In my case, the Haudenosaunee creation story tells us of women's esteemed status and of the responsibilities of men.[3] It tells us that we descended from Awen'ha'i, a woman who fell from the sky world through a hole in the ground where a standing tree had been uprooted. She landed on a turtle's back, bringing with her the medicines of tobacco and strawberries. On her arrival, it was the water beings that greeted and assisted Sky Woman. Awen'ha'i is believed to have subsequently given birth to a daughter, Gaende'so'k, or Zephyr, who in turn gave birth to twins, Sapling (the Creator) and an impatient Flint. The latter caused his mother's death by pushing his way out of her armpit to enter into the world. Gaende'so'k therefore became the first to die and be buried in the new earth world. Her burial is meaningful to us as *Ukwehuwé* (real human beings). Gaende'so'k is also the individual responsible for energizing Turtle Island (North America) with the eternal potential of Haudenosaunee existence.

Women are thus the very individuals through whom we trace our earliest origins and upon whom we continue to rely for continuity and survival. The three sisters – corn, beans, and squash – for instance, provide us with sustenance and nourishment. As Mohawk scholar Deborah Doxtator (1997, 32–33) writes, "Children born to the women created on the earth are referred to as the new faces pushing up from the earth. In the 'Thanksgiving Address' – a story that sets out the order of the universe – the earth is 'our mother who supports our feet.'" The creation story is key to understanding the esteemed status of women in my nation. After giving birth to twins, Gaende'so'k's spirit was released upon her death, and she became, literally, the progenitor of the nation. Indeed, this is where the word and very concept of *Yethi-nihstenha Onhwentsya* (she-to-us, our mother, the earth) comes from (S. Hill 2017, 21, 290). Women are fundamental to understanding our origins and continued existence as peoples. As ha dih nyoh writers Paul Williams and Curtis Nelson (1995, 20) write, "It is the women's function to bring forth and nurture life, just as the Earth does." Moreover, women's ability and potential to sustain humankind is continually affirmed through the very concept of "our mother, the earth" itself – a principle that is widely recognized, remembered, and acknowledged in ceremony, even today.

The importance of women, however, should not be misunderstood as deriving only from the story of creation. Indeed, women are central to the story of the Great Law of Peace, or Kayaneren'kowa, the very basis of our traditional constitution and governance as peoples.[4] The Kayaneren'kowa is regarded as a "gift from the Creator for the purpose of saving the people of the Six Nations from destroying themselves." It is understood as the "great, proper path" because, prior to the coming of the Great Law and the establishment of the Confederacy, it was a time of great sorrow and terror for Haudenosaunee. As Seneca scholar John Mohawk explains:

All order and safety had broken down completely and the
rule of the headhunter dominated the culture. When a man
or woman died ... the aggrieved family then sought vengeance and a member set forth with the purpose of finding [an] unsuspecting and arguably innocent offender and
exacting revenge. That killing sparked a spiral of vengeance
and reprisal which found assassins stalking the Northeast-
ern woodlands in a never-ending senseless bloodletting.

Mohawk describes the context out of which a young man
known to the Haudenosaunee as Ayenwahtha – the Great
Peacemaker – brought a message of peace to the people.
Brought to earth by Sapling – the Creator himself and son
of Gaende'so'k – the Peacemaker's message spoke of three
philosophical principles that would ease our terror on
Earth: peace, power, and righteousness, which he understood
in this way:

Righteousness means justice practiced between men and
between Nations; it means a desire to see justice prevail.
[Peace] means soundness of mind and body ... for that is
what comes when minds are sane and bodies are cared for.
Power means authority, the authority of law and custom,
backed by such force as is necessary to make justice prevail;
it means also religion, for justice enforced is the will of the
[Creator] and has his sanction.

Though the Peacemaker's message is thought to have taken
some time to reach the people and be accepted among them,
it came to our nations at a time of tremendous strife and
turmoil.

The message established a new system of governance, a
system that reinforced the role of women as "cultivators of
the soil, as leaders ... and as the holders of the future generations." Ayenwahtha is believed to have spread his words of

peace first to a female. This woman, Tsikonhsase, "lived along the warpath and had once benefited greatly from the wartime state." He spoke to her the words of peace, righteousness, and power, and when he finished, Tsikonhsase is believed to have accepted them. She also agreed to enforce the Peacemaker's great message. Ayenwahtha is believed to have stated: "Since you are the first to accept the [Great] Law of Peace ... I will declare that it shall be women who shall possess the title of Chieftainships. They shall name the Chiefs."

Thus, Haudenosaunee women are recognized as being fundamental to the Great Peace. Their status as holders of chiefly titles dates as far back as Kayaneren'kowa itself, esti- mated to have reached the Haudenosaunee in 1192, some eight hundred years before the United States of America would develop its own Constitution, which was informed by our Kayaneren'kowa (Johansen 1995).[5] Tsikonhsase was the very first Yakoyaner (clan mother). Governance among the Haudenosaunee was established and subsequently main- tained through her original clan status – a system of affiliation that has since been traced through one's mother, in my own case, Turtle Clan. Women quite literally enable political or- ganization, governance, and the clan system in my nation. In this role, they are responsible for the appointment (and depos- ition) of Confederacy chiefs. In short, women are of funda- mental importance to the future of the Haudenosaunee: as the original occupiers of Turtle Island and as clan mothers, they are the very basis of our governance as peoples. As Mohawk scholar Audra Simpson (2014, 48) writes, one's clan affiliation determined one's "place in the order of things."

The responsibility of establishing peace, however, is by no means the responsibility of women alone. In fact, the Great Peacemaker enlisted another helper on his journey. Follow- ing his visit to Tsikonhsase, the Great Peacemaker journeyed onward towards the Kahnawà:ke, or Mohawk Nation. There, he is believed to have met up with Tekarihoken, a Kanyen'kehà:ka man believed to have eaten humans. Ayenwahtha – the Great Peacemaker – spoke to him the words of peace, righteousness, and power, and when he finished, Tekarihoken is said to have accepted them. Tekarihoken also agreed to enforce the Peacemaker's great message. Because he was the first man to accept the Great Law of Peace, the Peacemaker made him the first *sachem* (leader) in the Mohawk Nation. Sachems have since been expected to uphold the message of peace and to practise a good mind.

In choosing two helpers, one male and the other female, the Great Peacemaker established a "duality between men and women, a balance" (Williams and Nelson 1995, 14). Women and men hold autonomous and separate responsibilities related to all aspects of life, including kinship, political organization, economic relations, and the division of labour. These responsibilities elevate the status of Haudenosaunee women but also demand the unanimity and "good mind" of male leaders. Indeed, we are responsible as men to think about maintaining a balance of genders. In the place of violence and warring, we are responsible for using the power of *Kanikonhri:yo* (good minds), brought to us by the Peacemaker, to be kind and supportive of one another and "to accomplish things together for the benefit of society" (R. Monture 2014, 9).

In this regard, maintaining the balance of the universe extends beyond men's and women's separate and distinct spheres. As ha dih nyoh scholar Barbara Mann (2000, 98) explains,

> Women have their own ceremonies, rituals, vision quests ... just as the men have theirs, but together, the community forms a healthy spiritual whole. Moreover, each half is always fully apprised of what the other half is doing which works to ensure that its own half fits snugly into the space left for it by its gendered complement. Men's councils await the decisions of women's councils. Women's

planting assesses the strength of men's hunting. Gendering
entirely permeates Iroquoian culture. It is twinship ... in
continual, human action.

Mann's assessment of gender relations and her use of the
word *twinship* to describe it is profound. It illustrates how
women's elevated status cannot be understood without com-
prehending the simultaneous and complementary status of
men (see Anderson 2000, 173–74). Balance is maintained,
in other words, through a dynamic interaction between men
and women maintaining Ukwehuwé existence.

The maintenance of gender balance and complementarity
actually demands that the roles, responsibilities, and ener-
gies of both Haudenosaunee men and women be embraced
now and into the future. As Marlyn Kane and Sylvia Maracle
(1989, 12) write, there are two interpermeable halves in
life – one female and the other male – and both halves
have to be there to make it complete (also see Anderson 2000,
173–74). The promotion of "balance and harmony in all
of our [human] relationships" (Alfred 1993, 8) is an all-
pervasive responsibility of the Haudenosaunee that stems
from the Creator's original instruction. This is most certainly
true of the relationships between men and women. In theor-
izing gender relations, Gerald Taiaiake Alfred (1993, 13–14)
writes: "There are twin responsibilities for men and women:
men must acknowledge, respect, and work to help eliminate
the heavy burden that women carry; and women must com-
mit themselves to making the nation livable from within the
culture. A continuing neglect of either one of these responsibilities will end the cycle of life as surely as any 'environmental catastrophe.'"

AS A HAUDENOSAUNEE man, I have a responsibility to maintain
the balance of the universe, a responsibility I see myself taking

on in writing this book. In recent decades, scholars, governments, and the courts have addressed gender discrimination in the Indian Act through progressive analyses, legislation, and judgments such as *McIvor v Canada* (2007) and the Gender Equity in Indian Registration Act, which followed on its heels in 2010. *McIvor* found that section 6 of the revised Indian Act perpetuated gender discrimination by giving fewer rights to the descendants of female Indians who had married non-Indians. In my case, because I was registered under section 6(2) of the Indian Act, I cannot pass on status to my children unless I marry a Status Indian. This is known as the two-generation cut off. By contrast, if the situation were reversed and it had been my father who had been a Status Indian and my mother the non-Indian, then I would have been entitled to status under section 6(1). If I married a non-Indian, my child would be entitled to status. Thus, three generations are given status. I refer to this as a legal phenomenon that affects people who are related as cousins (Cannon 2007a, 36).

McIvor and the Gender Equity in Indian Registration Act addressed sexism in the Indian Act, but they said nothing about racialization – the process whereby the original inhabitants of the land became "Indians," "Métis," or were denied federal recognition altogether (Andersen 2014; Cannon 2014; Lawrence 2012). Broadly speaking, *racialization* refers to a set of practices, beliefs, ways of thinking, and state recognition processes that have made Indianness compulsory. The courts and legislation sought to redress how my mother and her descendants had been discriminated against on the grounds of her gender, but they failed to address why it was that the Canadian state, rather than Indigenous law, should have the authority to determine her status in the first place.

Why is it that after more than 150 years of it being a nation Indigenous people are still dealing with Canada as "Indians?" Prior to colonization, Indigenous peoples were not "Indians," nor were our territories delimited to the lands "reserved" for Indians under settler law. We defined ourselves as distinct peoples and nations with vast territories, trade networks, treaty agreements, strategic and military alliances, and political relationships that were peoplehood-based and nation to nation. People became Indians so that the state could delimit the occupation of certain lands to Indians and the remainder to settlers. This process coincided with the view that Turtle Island was *terra nullius*, an empty, unoccupied land. It was through the sorting out of lands "set apart by Her Majesty for the use and benefit" of the Indians that the idea of whiteness, and indeed race, became concretized in what is now called Canada (Harris 1993; Lawrence 2002; Thobani 2007). Therefore, the category "Indian" is no more than a legal construction rooted in the doctrine of discovery and histories of land appropriation and colonial domination. It is the product of the unilateral power Canada granted *itself* under section 91(24) of the Constitution Act, 1867, to claim jurisdiction and then legislate over what it called "Indians."

In this book, I examine the role that sexism played in this process, and I argue that it is the responsibility of Indigenous nations and Indigenous men to understand that racialization and sexism are interlocked. Sexism dwells in and is safeguarded in patriarchy, which invaded our nations along with the colonizers, transforming what in many cases was largely egalitarianism into an imbalanced set of gender relations characterized by male dominance in family, cultural, and political life (Cannon and Sunseri 2017, xiv; Code 2000, 378). This is not to say that all Indigenous nations were egalitarian; indeed, some were patrilineal and patriarchal. However, the type of patriarchy that was imposed – European heteropatriarchy – was different. It was rooted in religiously authorized ethnocentrism and monotheistic exclusivism, and it normalized heterosexuality as a mode of gender oppression (see Mariedaughter 1986; Penelope 1986; Trebilcot 1988).

Heteropatriarchy informed the process of establishing the category "Indian" and erasing nation-based understandings of gender, sexuality, identity, and ancestry. In settler Indian policy, women were assumed to be the appendages of men when it came to marriage and Indianness. This assumption followed from Western heteropatriarchal and capitalist notions of women as the property of their husbands. Under the status provisions of the Indian Act, women therefore lost and acquired federal recognition based on the race of the man they married. Consequently, Indianness was premised on a patrilineal model of descent reckoning common to Europeans in the mid-nineteenth century. The criteria used to determine who was – and who was not – an Indian was also rooted in early race-based thinking about blood quantum and in colonial histories that did not recognize linguistic and cultural differences among Indigenous groups (see Kauanui 2008; Tallbear 2013). In her book, *Hawaiian Blood*, J. Kehaulani Kauanui (2008, 11) observes that systems of federal recognition based on blood quantum were "specifically devised to quantify ancestry in the service of discourses of dilution, which then lend themselves to the discounting narratives of assimilation"; they were used in the present and the past "to appropriate Native lands and to promote cultural and biological assimilation." Blood quantum logic undermined our genealogical connections to our lands and reduced sovereign nations to the status of racial minorities (Cannon and Sunseri 2011; Porter 1999).

Patriarchy and sexism influenced the regime of band council government in Canada, which conferred status and decision making on men. In the case of the Haudenosaunee, the result was particularly damaging. As Alfred (2014, 77) writes, "If you're trying to steal someone's land, you have to go after the owners, and in the Haudenosaunee community, the owners, it so happened, were the females. So you put those two together, and it's a pretty compelling reason to go after the traditional roles of women in our society." Under the Indian Act, it was assumed and expected that band council governments – appointed by an all-male Indian electorate until 1951 – would administer and enforce gender inequality. It went without question that only men would vote in band council elections. Not surprisingly, the imposition of patriarchal governance structures created an element of hostility and sex discrimination in Indigenous communities that has yet to be reversed.

That the colonial enterprise of racism was inseparable from heterosexism and patriarchy is not a new idea. Where the Indian Act is concerned specifically, ha dih nyoh scholars Thomas Isaac and Mary Sue Maloughney (1992) suggest that colonial ideas and assumptions about Indianness and femaleness literally combined to make Indigenous women unequal by virtue of both their gender and racialization. At the level of common sense, it was assumed that a woman, along with her children, would take on the racial status of her husband at marriage. In this sense, the racialization of Indigenous peoples could not have been realized in Canada without sexism and Western patriarchal knowledge. It went unsaid that women should be subject to the male-dominated, hierarchically structured Indian Act, with band council governments carrying out Western patriarchal customs and law. The patriarchy administered by band council governments, as Audra Simpson (2014, 61) has noted, was further consolidated by "fears of the world outside, the fears of the power white men may carry, and fears of the further dissolution of territory."

Indigenous scholars have also demonstrated that sexism has been used to exact, mobilize, and entrench colonial dominance, legal assimilation, and what Australian writer and historian Patrick Wolfe (2006, 388) has referred to as the elimination of the Native: "As opposed to enslaved people, whose reproduction augmented their owners' wealth, Indigenous people obstructed settlers' access to land, so their increase was counterproductive. In this way, the restrictive racial classification of Indians straightforwardly furthered the logic of elimination" (see also Kauanui 2008; Palmater 2015; Tallbear 2013). As scholars of settler colonialism like Wolfe have shown, the objective has always been either to eliminate us legislatively and physically or to assimilate or acculturate us by making us into "civilized," "white," or "British" citizens. The logic of elimination was an organizing principle of settler colonial society, and the act of federal recognition or forced citizenship must be understood as something other (or perhaps greater) than "the generality of non-colonial genocides" (Wolfe 2006, 400).[6]

Proponents of Indigenous feminism have also documented and drawn attention to the interconnectedness of sexism and racialization (see also Monture-Angus 1995; Turpel 1993). Beverley Jacobs (2014), a Mohawk scholar, for instance, defines patriarchy as none other than an attack on Indigenous womanhood following from colonization that has enabled a continued violence to be enacted on the bodies of Indigenous women. And scholars in queer studies have pointed out Indian policy is based on the heteropatriarchal assumption that we, as Indians, will marry members of the opposite sex (Cannon 1998; Mariedaughter 1986; Penelope 1986; Trebilcot 1988). Indeed, the limitations placed upon me as a result of my categorization under section 6(2) meant that I not only have to be concerned about the race or status of the person I marry but also about their gender if I want to bequeath Indian status to my children.

My book builds upon these arguments by showing that sexism in the Indian Act doesn't affect just women and gay or transgendered Indigenous people – it affects all Indigenous people and nations. Indeed, Indigenous feminists argue that racialized and Indigenous men participate in their own continued subordination even when they oppose racism (and colonial dispossession) because patriarchy is left unchallenged (see Dhamoon 2015, 29–31; Fellows and Razack 1998; Razack 1999, 13–14). To back up and put all this in simpler terms, the Indian Act made Indian women and their children unequal to Indian men and their children, and the impact of sexism on Status Indian communities cannot be underestimated. For women, marriage to an unregistered or non-Indian man meant that they and their children were stripped legally of all statutory entitlements normally afforded to Status Indians. Upon marriage, they were banished from reserve communities. They held no further right to live on a reserve, to share in the property or collective assets of their bands, to hunt or fish, to access education and health care provisions, or to be buried in their home communities alongside their ancestors. Many women relocated to cities because of federal legislation, including laws that fell short of addressing the distribution of matrimonial property upon dissolution of marriage. Accustomed as they became to notions of interpersonal and institutionalized male dominance, women faced a formidable sexism directed at them by band councils and their communities. For men who retained Indian status and who remained on reserves, their racialization as Indians transformed social relations so that women were seen – though not always – as outsiders. The Indian Act created and legitimized the conviction that those who had "married out" represented a threat to Indigenous communities. When Indian status provisions combined with sexist attitudes about the "illegitimacy" of children, the election of male-only band councils, and male-only governance, the effects of patriarchy were especially damaging and intense.

The Indian Act also made Indian women unequal to settler women and their descendants under an imposed and legislatively sanctioned system of racialization. Until 1985, non-Indigenous women, as wives of Indian men, acquired federal recognition as Indians and, in many cases, they have lived and participated in our reserve communities for generations. Indian women have been discriminated against as women, and they have been discriminated against as Indians. It is therefore clearly incorrect to describe the inequality that Indigenous women have faced as deriving only from sexism. Ultimately, the interlocking systems of sexism and racism have placed Indigenous men and women at a disadvantage relative to settler populations, the state, the legal system, and to each other.

Taken together, sexism and racialization have formed the principal instrument of power that has been used (and is continuing to be used) to disrupt the balance of gender complementarity in Indigenous communities (Cannon 2007a, 2007b; Sunseri 2011). As forms of discrimination, sexism and racialization do not simply impact Indigenous people as either "women" or "Indians." The sexism directed at Indigenous women through the Indian Act belongs collectively to all "Indians," women and men. Sexism therefore undermines the collective rights of Indigenous nations. I call on Canadian courts, lawmakers, and settler and Indigenous governments to stop telling a raceless story of sexism, one that envisages Indian women as divisible into either/or terms. This way of thinking restricts the possibilities for challenging sexism. Sexism does not belong to women alone – it threatens to define, reduce, and ultimately extinguish the registered Indian population. This either/or thinking prevents Indigenous nations from reconciling the treatment of Indian women, their children, and others who have been excluded from the category "Indian" and involuntarily enfranchised. I also call on Indigenous men to explore the complex ways in which their life's journey has been shaped by the heterosexual patriarchy directed at Indigenous women – at their mothers and grandmothers. I call on them to think about how they have been complicit in it and what they can do to return us to a state of balance. Writing this book was part of my own journey.

TO SPEAK AS A MAN is important to me, as my (cis)gender defines my sense of self and belonging. To say that I am male, Oneida, and Haudenosaunee means that I am conscious of early treaties, such as the Haldimand Deed of 1784, the Simcoe Treaty, the Silver Chain, and the Guswentah (or Two Row Wampum), which state who we are as Indigenous nations and as citizens and which describe our relationship with Canadian settlers. It also means that I am aware of the traditional stories we tell ourselves about women's esteemed status and about matrilineal kinship organization as it was brought to us by the Great Peacemaker. To say that I am Haudenosaunee means that there is an ancient, and not just a scholarly, context for opposing sexism and patriarchy.

Indigenous men typically do not talk about the presence or history of sex discrimination or the way it has impacted our lives, but there are important exceptions. Indeed, it would be overly reductive to suggest that all Indian men have passively corroborated the patriarchal systems of power that were imposed on us by the early settler state. In the absence of research and documentation, we can't assume that all the male children of involuntary enfranchised women – men such as myself – supported the sexist provisions of the Indian Act. We know that some men refused to support the disinheritance and banishment of women and children from their communities (Jamieson 1978, 13; Jamieson 1986, 121; Weaver 1974, 52–53; also see Weaver 1983, 60). In my own nation, Susan Hill, a Kanyen'kehaka scholar, has drawn on archival evidence to show that the Confederacy Council disagreed with "Dominion attempts to claim authority over lands and membership in this manner." They opposed the imposition of patriarchal systems of legal enfranchisement and attempts to undermine "family structures established under the Kayaneren'kowa" (S. Hill 2017, 192, 199, 227). It would seem that many men in my community at Grand River Territory remembered the ancient systems of knowledge about women's roles as leaders, including the role they played in social life, governance, and clan-based kinship organization. Other men openly welcomed women back to reserve communities after the Indian Act was amended in 1985 (Woodward 1986, 3). And in the 1990s, the Assembly of Manitoba Chiefs recognized that "full self-government is the opportunity to overcome patriarchy, not an excuse for its continuation" (Greschner 1992, 348).

The nonpatriarchal characteristics demonstrated by Ukwehuwé men in early Confederacy Councils should be adopted today by the coming generation of men, especially when it comes to thinking about women as "the critical identity holders of the nation" (Antone 2015, 22). As Bob Antone argues in "Reconstructing Indigenous Male Thought," we must revisit these early principles if we are ever "to shed the colonial cloak of Western masculinity" (23). We must revisit and think more about our own systems of knowledge as men and Haudenosaunee peoples. On the one hand, this means looking to the stories we have told each other as Indigenous nations, especially about our responsibilities as men and women, for generations. As Antone suggests of the creation story and the story of the Great Law, "our psyche has to accept those teachings if we are going to decolonize" (23). The idea of men working to uphold the balance of the nation is especially significant to our future as Haudenosaunee peoples, especially if one considers the work of Onyota'a:ka scholar Lina Sunseri (2011), who writes that "being again of one mind" will require a commitment on behalf of both men and women to be mindful of and dismantle settler colonial dominance and heteropatriarchy.

Although some men understand and accept their responsibilities and support the rights of Indian women, the tendency among the majority has been to divorce race and gender discrimination, to allow the rights of the Indian collective to eclipse the rights of Indian women. This tendency has kept us Indigenous men and nations from developing a more enlightened, urgent, and decolonizing politics. Indeed, the tendency has become so broad that it is not uncommon to hear some Indigenous women – some of whom may identify as Indigenous feminists – talk of the greater "self-evidence" of racism over sexism (Hammersmith 1992, 56–57; LaChapelle 1982, 262). This tendency has prevented us from undoing the citizenship injustice of the Indian Act, from dismantling the legal and conceptual regime of Indianness.

We can no longer afford a "race to innocence" where the patriarchal attitudes we have learned as a result of colonization and the Indian Act are concerned (see Fellows and Razack 1998; Razack 1999, 13–14). Indeed, I hope this book shows that the reason we need to dismantle Indian Act patriarchy and sexism is not so that we can "be nice" to Indigenous women (see Andrea Smith, quoted in Khan, Hugill, and McCreary 2010, 42) but because heteropatriarchy is a system of colonial dominance and oppression that seeks to obliterate our very existence as Indigenous people. It seeks to reverse our stories – in my own case, the story of creation and the coming of the Great Law. As Indigenous men, we should never, ever, forget this.

To be clear, I do not mean to come up with a series of prescriptive practices for engaging with Indigenous masculinity in this book. Indeed, the concept of masculinity is itself a highly gendered social construction, one that stems from European property law and patriarchal power. I do not suggest that there is one particular version (or "story") of Indigenous masculinity – or even that I am remotely an adequate spokesperson to define or lead this scholarship. Nor do I mean to suggest that we shouldn't problematize the concept of masculinity as Eurocentric and cisgendered (see

Halberstam 1998; Tatonetti 2015). Rather, I want to look inward at my own experience of colonial dominance and propose that it is indeed possible to "story" and indeed "restory" Indian Act patriarchy. It is possible to move beyond a colonial and decidedly Eurocentric way of thinking in singular terms about gender, sex discrimination, Indigenous masculinity, and the impact of sexism on entire nations of people.

IN THIS BOOK, I restory the Indian Act by exploring how the separation of racism and sexism unfolded historically, particularly how the last four decades of Canadian case law and politics have influenced the Indian Act and Indian status provisions. This book is not meant to be an exhaustive account of all that has happened since the 1970s. Other voices have spoken about these matters. Here, I am presenting my own set of perspectives as a Status Indian who, like so many others, has been treated differently and unequally in relation to other Indians because of discriminatory policies. I speak as a citizen of the Oneida Nation whose familial roots lie with the Six Nations of Grand River Territory. I also speak as a man exploring questions of sexism, heteropatriarchy, masculinity, and power, as a man exploring the benefits of using an anticolonial, decolonizing, and feminist Indigenous framework to interpret our complex personal and historical pasts. In writing this book, my intention is to create a space from which we can begin to realize an anticolonial and antisexist literature written by men affected by sexism. I believe a space for the emergence of this work can come from Indigenous men whose mothers have been targeted as Indian women, from men whose first thinking about sexism was motivated by the fact that they were Indigenous, and not simply because of feminist theory (Cannon 2011).

In Chapter 1, I provide a historical overview of the Indian Act and Indian policy. Chapter 2 then concentrates on the

1970s, comparing the two well-known constitutional challenges of the day: the *Drybones* and *Lavell* cases. The criteria
that was used to determine whether these cases centred on
race or sex discrimination set a legal (if not ontological precedent) for seeing Status Indians as either women or Indians,
but never both. I also reveal how legislation in this decade
made it possible for women and their descendants to be treated
as individuals who threatened to undermine the collective. I
document resistance by the National Indian Brotherhood in
particular because it illuminates how Indigenous identity and
citizenship were understood, constrained, and contested at
the time.

Chapter 3 concentrates on the 1980s and '90s, opening
with a description of the limitations, or residual discrimination, of the 1985 amendments to the Indian Act. It addresses
how this discrimination left some Indian women and bands
supporting the Charter of Rights and Freedoms as a viable
option for the resolution of human rights grievances, including intergroup rights issues arising from legislated discrimination. I also show how some Status Indian organizations
opposed all use or application of the Charter, going so far
as to mobilize against it in the name of both culture and
"tradition." My intention in this chapter is to illuminate how
histories of racialization and sexism came to structure the
activities of Indian political organizations in the 1980s and
1990s, in turn producing a bifurcated politics and a way of
thinking about identity, belonging, and citizenship.

In Chapter 4, I bring the historical discussion full circle by
focusing on the *McIvor* case. I argue that even after four decades, the courts and Parliament continue to see Indian women
in either/or terms. I take the position that, in Canada, the
very first act of colonial injustice was racialized injustice, re-
ferring to none other than the process through which we
became Indians under section 91(24) of the Constitution Act,
1867. I suggest that until this history is reconciled, we cannot

engage in a productive or otherwise transformative discussion about Indigenous identity and citizenship in Canada. I argue that race matters, but that, as a concept, it is not being disentangled from nationhood. This, in turn, detracts from any critical engagement with the history of settler colonialism and the racialized processes whereby we are imagined to have become Indians in the first place.

My intention throughout is to highlight the challenges and complexities surrounding the politics of identity and recognition and to provide a series of new insights with respect to the invigoration and renavigation of them. Racism strikes at the very core of our experience as Indigenous peoples in Canada. Our lives are marked by these histories, including but not limited to matters of Indianness, the Indian Act, racial profiling, missing and murdered women, poverty, and economic marginalization. As an Indigenous person, and as a Status Indian (that is, a racialized person), I believe that Indigenous peoples must develop and share a vocabulary to describe histories of racism and the lived realities of Indigenous peoples in Canada. We cannot hope to witness or bring about a change in the structure of settler colonialism without providing these tools to one another and our nations.

In calling attention to race matters, I am not suggesting that stories of racialization ought to replace or even overshadow stories of sexism. Nor am I suggesting that Indigenous peoples should struggle as or be seen as racial minorities. I follow the Seneca scholar Rob Porter (1999), who insists on drawing a distinction between Indigenous peoples and ethnic or racial groups in light of our history and sovereignty as nations. Several other Indigenous scholars have suggested that we should refuse the invitation to Canadian citizenship at every turn (see Alfred 2005; Cannon and Sunseri 2011, xix–xx, 265; Henderson 2002; Porter 1999, 154–58). While I agree, I am also mindful that we cannot help but be concerned with matters of race as Indigenous peoples because of the way it has been so fundamentally tied to colonial injustice from the beginning. For better or worse, colonialism – mutated as it has been through the racialized construct of "Indian" attached to colonialism – shapes the everyday experience of, and politics involving, Indigenous peoples in Canada.

Racism cannot be fully understood in Canada, nor citizenship injustices reconciled, so long as Indigenous peoples are administered as "Indians" under federal legislation. Indianness embodies a way of thinking about identity, citizenship, nationhood, and fiduciary relationships in state-based and racialized terms. As a matter of routine, we are pulled into a political relationship with Canada as "Indians," or as "Aboriginal" peoples, but not as nations (Alfred 2005, 23; Alfred and Corntassel 2005, 599; Coulthard 2007). These politics work to expunge histories of colonial dominance aimed at our nations through the very act of renaming. The word *Indian*, and the politics surrounding it, should therefore be resisted at every turn. In fact, it is important to think critically about what is accomplished ideologically, and in terms of the maintenance of colonialism, each time we employ the category "Indian." In this book, I use the word *Indian* in a descriptive sense, as a term that is deeply attached to the legislative history of settler colonialism in Canada, established in the first instance of the *Indian Act*. I do not use *Indian* as an identity to which we ought to aspire.

In other words, in order to undo citizenship injustice, we need to dismantle the legal and conceptual regime of Indianness. We need to acknowledge Indigenous peoples not as citizens of Canada, or as Indians, for that matter, but as nations. I hope this book will help to facilitate and further an understanding of these issues, paving the way for a new politics of Indian identity and citizenship. Indeed, I hope it will inspire research that recognizes that at the time of contact there were no "Indians" living on Turtle Island – only diverse nations of peoples. I hope my contribution might in some way invigorate the thinking that goes into knowing and defining ourselves as dynamic and resilient Ukwehuwé, as people who can at once accommodate ha dih nyoh and other settler populations in our communities and reject the legislative categories of belonging imposed on us by the state.

The Indian Act, a Legacy
of Racist Patriarchy

RACIALIZATION AND SEXISM worked together through colonialism to define and structure the political reality of Status Indians in Canada. Racism was realized, at first, through taken-for-granted attitudes about Indianness and, later, through legislative rules about Indian women, marital status, and intermarriage. These colonial injustices (injustices realized through sexist, white, and European patriarchal understandings about women and gender) began before Confederation. Early missionaries understood themselves to be responsible for "civilizing" Indigenous populations, for indoctrinating them in the Christian ethos and patriarchal kinship structures. When Paul Le Jeune, a Jesuit missionary, observed egalitarian relations between men and women among the Montagnais-Naskapi Nations in what some now call Eastern Canada, he wrote: "The women have great power here. A man may promise you something, and if he does not keep his promise, he thinks he is sufficiently excused when he tells you that his wife did not wish him to do it. I told him then that he was the master, and that in France women do not rule their husbands (Brodribb 1984, 88).

The patriarchal views expressed by early missionaries such as Le Jeune were upheld throughout the period of the fur trade in the sixteenth and early seventeenth centuries (Andersen 2014, 44–49, 181). Indeed, during this time, a system of Eurocentric patriarchy was perpetuated in the New World, striking, as Andrea Bear Nicholas (1994, 230) writes, "at the heart of Native cultures, their values of sharing and cooperation, and their corresponding lack of any concept of private property." The European idea of womanhood, which revolved around gender inequality and female domesticity, was also re-affirmed (Stevenson 1999, 55; see also Smith 2005b). Europeans assumed that women were subordinate to men or, at the very least, that their sexuality and labour power were things to be commodified and treated as male private property (Stevenson 1999, 54). As historian Sylvia Van Kirk (1980, 88) writes in *Many Tender Ties,* "Despite her important contributions and influence in certain areas, the Indian woman in fur trade society was at the mercy of a social structure devised primarily to meet the needs of European males." The relentless European pursuit of empire and nationhood meant that Indigenous peoples were subjected to recurrent campaigns to refashion their social structures in the colonizer's image. The racism that underpinned both the fur trade and missionary campaigns could not have been realized were it not for sexism.

The attitudes of fur traders and missionaries carried over into the political discourse of the late nineteenth century. Consider the words of Sir Hector Langevin, an early imperialist who, in 1876, expressed a claim to European superiority while simultaneously revealing an ideology of paternalism and sexist male supremacy: "Indians were not in the same position as white men. As a rule they had no education, and they were like children to a very great extent. They, therefore, required a great deal more protection than white men" (J.R. Miller 1989, 191). Similarly, Alexander Morris, who was responsible for making treaties with Indigenous peoples on the Prairies, pronounced: "Let us have Christianity and civilization to leaven the masses of heathenism and paganism among the Indian Tribes; let us have a wise and paternal government faithfully carrying out the provisions of our treaties ... They are wards of Canada, let us do our duty by them" (Frideres 1983, 2).

The sentiments expressed by Langevin and Morris betrayed the paternalistic and highly gendered intentions behind Canada's Indian policy, which had solidified by the early nineteenth century. The implementation of the reserve system in Upper Canada during the 1830s was the keystone to all later policy (Tobias 1983, 41). The surface motivation for the system was to enforce "British-agricultural-Christian patterns of behaviour upon Native communities" (Frideres 1983, 22; see also Jamieson 1978, 1986), but at a deeper level, the initiative was underpinned by the "commonsense" racist and sexist ideologies of the colonizers. In short, the reserve system was intended to resocialize "Indians" (Tobias 1983, 41). Seen as an inferior race of people susceptible to "nomadism," "corruption," "laziness," and "vice," Indians were thought to need spiritual direction and the assistance of the newcomers. Their salvation, it was believed, would come under the auspices of a superior race of European men.

The implementation of the reserve system made invidious distinctions between men and women. Reserve lands – Crown lands reserved for the sole use and benefit of Indians – would be owned by male Indians, which resulted in significant financial, legal, emotional, and psychological strains and losses by women upon divorce from their husbands (Montour 1987; Bastien 2008). Early federal Indian policy sought to construct – and uphold – hierarchies of gender in reserve communities. Reserves were "internal colonies" – social laboratories intended to restructure and eliminate the egalitarian gender relations that had existed in many Indigenous communities prior to European contact (Stevenson 1999, 65). Fuelled by racist beliefs about the inferiority of Indians and the superiority of early white settlers and by patriarchal ideas about women, the reserve system (which remains today) targeted our (grand) mothers in the sense that the goal was to resocialize them, both as Indians and as women.

A more aggressive trend towards the imposition of patriarchy and our assimilation and racialization as peoples occurred in the 1850s. In 1857, Upper Canada passed An Act to Encourage the Gradual Civilization of the Indian Tribes in This Province, and to Amend the Laws Respecting Indians. The statute is commonly known as the Gradual Civilization Act. This legislation followed An Act for the Better Protection of the Lands and Property of the Indians of Lower Canada, which had been introduced in what is now Quebec in 1850 (Magnet 2003, 42, 45). The titles of both acts reveal their colonial inspiration and symbolize the first instance of Indianness in Canada. One of the central features of the 1857 legislation was enfranchisement, with the explicit and avowed purpose of legally assimilating Indians. The premise was simple: Indian men, upon meeting certain criteria (they were literate, free of debt, and of good moral character) could (along with their dependants) give up legal "Indian status" and become "persons." Thus, Indian men would be accorded the rights and privileges held by every ordinary, "civilized" Euro-Canadian (Tobias 1983, 42). The titles and underlying premise of these statutes reveal more about whiteness than they do about Indigenous identities (Brownlie 2006; Razack 2002). They represent the material and symbolic work that goes into producing a white settler society. They are also symbolic of the act of forcing Canadian citizenship on Indigenous peoples (Porter 1999). Indian legislation, in other words, is premised on racism, on the idea that it is only in becoming a non-Indian that one can attain personhood. By default, the only true persons are white settlers, a historical injustice that has yet to be reconciled. As "Indians," Indigenous people were not recognized as persons or as nations of people (Turner 2006).

Indian policy imposed the idea of Indianness on Indigenous peoples along with the idea of property ownership, a distinctly European notion rooted in the interests of capitalist accumulation and established in Canada through fur trade mercantilism (Bourgeault 1983). Indian policy was premised on disruptive and inherently patriarchal presumptions about kinship organization in Indigenous communities. The laws of enfranchisement dictated that our (grand)mothers would adopt the racialized status of their husbands, as would the men's children or dependants. Racialization meant the disempowerment of women and Indigenous children of both sexes. The goal was to impose a patrilineal method of descent reckoning. For many Indigenous communities, Indian policy threatened to fundamentally reorganize matrilineal and matrilocal kinship structures. The sexism that our (grand) mothers faced was clearly an effect of racialization and policies aimed at our legal assimilation as peoples.

Ideological or commonsense notions of racist patriarchy were reaffirmed two years after Confederation, in 1869, when Canada passed An Act for the Gradual Enfranchisement of Indians, the Better Management of Indian Affairs, and to Extend the Provisions of the Act 31st Victoria, Chapter 42, more commonly known as the Gradual Enfranchisement Act. The act introduced European-style elections to Indigenous communities. Under the act, elected band councils were empowered to make bylaws and, upon approval of the superintendent of the newly established Department of Indian Affairs, to deal with all minor concerns. The goal was to re-socialize Indians into a political system deemed superior and more responsible by settler colonists, to expedite the creation of hierarchical authority within communities by fostering a politics of dependency and by breaking down previous forms of decision making based on consensus. (It should be noted that the elective system was optional until 1895, when the government delegated to itself the authority to depose chiefs and councillors of bands not following the system. This amendment represented the most serious infringement on traditional forms of governance and remains in place today.)[1]

The act perpetuated previously initiated gender hierarchies, and it was simultaneously racist and patriarchal. Section 6 stipulated that Indigenous women who married non-Indian or unregistered men lost legal status as Indians, along with their children. As Mohawk activist Kathleen Jamieson (1986, 118) writes, "the statute of 1869, especially section 6 ... embodied the principle that, like other women, Indian women should be subject to their husbands." Our (grand)mothers were targeted by the Canadian state for different and unequal treatment. They were singled out and forced to relinquish federal and treaty recognition when they married non-Indians or when they married persons unable to register because of racial criteria in the Indian Act and early policies concerning "half breeds" (Campbell 1973).

The legislation also stipulated that band councils be elected by the male members of each federally recognized community. This meant that, for those who participated (or who had no other choice but to participate) in this kind of government, women were excluded (at least in an official sense) from having a voice in elections or in newly devised governance procedures. Women did not officially gain the right to participate in the elective system of governance until 1951, when Bill C-79 granted them the right to vote in band council elections (Jamieson 1986, 122). But, by then, some communities had already been following an elective system of governance for over eighty years. The memory of traditional government and gender balance was disrupted, if not lost, during that time. This was a serious infringement on structures of kinship and governance in communities, particularly in nations such as the Haudenosaunee where Indigenous women held enormous political influence, including the ability to appoint, and depose, hereditary chiefs. In fact, in the case of the Oneida, the influence of women extended well beyond political power: they could exercise sexual autonomy, divorce, own property, counsel or end wars, produce military supplies, decide the fate of prisoners, and adopt members of other nations (Sunseri 2011, 71; see also Alfred 1999; Goodleaf 1995; B. Mann 2008; Monture-Angus 1995; Stevenson 1999).

TO APPRECIATE THE history of colonial governance and interference and its impact on Indian women's status, it's worthwhile to consider my own community, the Six Nations at Grand River Territory, in more detail. Grand River Territory is unique, for example, in having evaded all requirements for an elective system of governance until October 7, 1924. As Mohawk scholar Rick Monture (2014, 17) writes: "In spite of the Crown's desire to subjugate the Haudenosaunee in their new lands, the Confederacy Council remained in place until 1924, albeit under the ever-watchful eye of the local Indian Agent on the reserve. Up to that time ... the Six Nations at Grand River Territory had been able to maintain a substantial portion of their traditional culture despite mounting pressures to assimilate into mainstream Canadian society." On October 7, however, and for reasons that lie far outside the scope of this book, the Royal Canadian Mounted Police stormed our hereditary council house (invalidating 141 years of the council's authority by settler colonial decree) and permanently padlocked the doors (see Cannon 2004, 201; S. Hill 2017, 236; R. Monture 2014, 17). A proclamation was posted on the council house door announcing the dissolution of that council and that a band council election would be held on October 21.

In terms of governance, our perseverance as Haudenosaunee was rooted in the rich history of oral tradition and culture at Grand River Territory. Our resistance to assimilative forms of governance stemmed, in other words, from the "sustained power of the stories that are at the foundation of Haudenosaunee philosophical thought" (R. Monture 2014, 17). The role that respect for women played in our perseverance has not been explored fully (Cannon 2004). For Haudenosaunee women, the decision to impose an elected system on the Six Nations would have been revolutionary. As the heads of matrilineages, they possessed all titles to chieftainships, they bestowed clan membership onto male children, and they appointed hereditary chiefs to the Confederacy Council. When the elected council became the only form of government recognized by the Canadian state, the Confederacy government ceased to be recognized (at least officially, in the eyes of Canada) as the basis of Six Nations governance.

How did these changes affect Haudenosaunee women and the attitudes of Haudenosaunee men in particular? The events of 1924 have been interpreted by outsiders as the beginnings of colonial intrusion and injustice (see Wright 1992, 324–25) and of Canadian government interference and reform-based movements at Grand River Territory (see Wright 1992; Shimony 1994). Although well-intentioned, these interpretations fail to connect political change with sexism and the transformation of women's status. By contrast, men in my own nation offered a different interpretation to the Standing Committee on Indian Self-Government in 1983:

> Since the inception of the various Indian Acts ... the Indian Act and the band council system has divided our people ... In introducing the elective band council system, the Canadian government saw itself as more democratic than traditional governments and ignored the role of the people and the clans, the women and the chiefs, in Haudenosaunee society. *The Haudenosaunee had serious problems with the Indian "advancement" sections and the elective band council*

system [because] they did not allow for the participation of women (they could not be on the band council, or vote) ... In each of the Haudenosaunee communities ... there were strong objections to even the possibility of the imposition of the Indian "advancement" provisions. The very concept of the Dominion government of Canada making laws that would govern the Haudenosaunee was most unacceptable to the Confederacy.[2]

According to the testimony, the Confederacy had voiced opposition to the elective system that had (at least on paper) replaced the traditional government at Six Nations at the expense and exclusion of women. In its appeal to justice, the Confederacy did not distinguish between imposed racialized governance and sexism (Cannon 1995). Instead, its members proposed a multidimensional understanding of historical events, one in which imposed racist governance structures could not be realized without sexism. This understanding should inform all histories of the imposition of the elective system in my nation and, more generally, Indigenous nations throughout Canada.

However, evidence suggests that some men in my nation had started to be socialized into patriarchal ways of thinking and knowing – regardless of their nation's memory, traditional law, and teachings about gender balance and complementarity. Consider, for example, a poem written by an "ardent Dehorner," Nelson Moses, which was published in 1908 in the Caledonia, Ontario, newspaper the *Haldimand Banner* and reprinted in 1972 without an inkling of analysis or interpretation in Sally Weaver's *Medicine and Politics among the Grand River Iroquois*. The poem, in which Moses expresses his opposition to the hereditary chiefs, is testimony to the subtle way in which reform-based efforts to dismantle the Confederacy from within my own community were grounded in hostility towards women:

Ye rusty chiefs all born that way
Your grannies say, you must obey
Altho' they think you know so much
Don't fool yourselves your but a bautch
The rusty chiefs, no judgement have
Who sit they there on whose behalf?
For granny's choice and granny's pride
Rules a nation, "unsatisfied." (Weaver 1972, 26)

Moses might not have intended to invoke opposition to women's influence and status in this poem. Yet, in opposing the Confederacy's chiefs and council, he was unable to avoid expressing his opposition towards the power of "grannies" to appoint chiefs. Put simply, his opposition to the hereditary council had patriarchal connotations. At the very least, Moses's poem provides a glimpse into the interconnectedness of opposition to hereditary governance and emerging patriarchal beliefs about women. I would also suggest that his comments illustrate that Indigenous communities were losing the social, legislative, and structural means to revitalize non-patriarchal memories and practices.

THE PROCESS BY WHICH Indigenous peoples were resocialized into Western racist patriarchal thought continued in the 1870s, when Canada passed the first legislation titled "the Indian Act."[3] The statute consolidated all previous policy concerning Indians into one piece of legislation. The act was all-encompassing and oppressive, as Frances Henry and Carol Tator (2006, 115) so eloquently describe in the *Colour of Democracy: Racism in Canadian Society:*

The *Indian Act* ... is the legislation that has intruded on the lives and cultures of Status Indians more than any other law. Though amended repeatedly, the Act's fundamental provisions have scarcely changed. They give the

state powers that range from defining how one is born or naturalized into "Indian" status to administering the estate of an Aboriginal person after death ... The Act gave Parliament control over Indian political structures, land-holding patterns, and resource and economic development. It covered almost every important aspect of the daily lives of Aboriginal peoples on reserves. The overall effect was to subject Aboriginal people to the almost unfettered rule of federal bureaucrats. The Act imposed non-Aboriginal forms of traditional governance, landholding practices, and cul-
· tural practices.

Like preceding legislation, the 1876 Indian Act imposed descent through the male line. Section 6 became section 3(c), which stipulated that, upon marriage to a non-Indian, a woman would "cease to be an Indian within the meaning of this Act." Section 3 clarified that the "term Indian means First. Any male person of Indian blood reputed to belong to a particular band; Secondly. Any child of such person; Thirdly. Any woman who is or was lawfully married to such person."

Major changes to the Indian Act that affected women were common after 1876. The Federal Franchise Act of 1885 extended the right to vote in federal elections to all Indian men but not to Indian women (Jamieson 1986). Section 26(2) of the 1927 Indian Act stipulated that "the Superintendent-General shall be the sole and final judge as to the moral character of the widow of any intestate Indian."[4] The section required that an Indian widow be of "good moral character" in order to receive an inheritance. Indian women could also be dispossessed of band royalties and inheritances upon the dissolution of a marriage if they failed to meet the character requirement. The assessment of a woman's character was done at the discretion of a paternalistic, non-Indigenous bureaucrat.

Until 1951, if an Indian woman married out, she remained on the band list and retained the right to continue collecting annuities and band moneys, even though she was no longer an "Indian," as defined by the Indian Act (Jamieson 1986, 122). Section 15(1)(a) of the 1951 Indian Act abolished this possibility. It stated that a woman who had married out was entitled only to a "one per capita share of the capital and revenue moneys held by His Majesty on behalf of the band."[5] Thus, upon marrying out, Indian women not only lost status, they lost band rights and privileges. In *Bill-31: Equality or Disparity?*, Joan Holmes (1987, 18) describes the advantages of band membership:

> A band member has the right to live on her/his band's reserve, to vote in band elections, to seek election as band chief or councillor, to own or inherit property and be buried on the reserve, and to have a share of income from band resources such as timber dues, sale of surrendered lands, and oil and gas revenues. A band member will also be eligible for on-reserve housing, health services, welfare and education assistance, to the extent that these services are available.

In essence, section 15(1)(a) required that an Indian woman be disenfranchised and disinherited from her own band when she married a non-Indian or unregistered person. It made enforcing patriarchal relations and practices an imperative of elected band councils, and it ensured that resentment over the loss of these status and rights would be directed not towards the Indian Act but towards Status Indians.

In 1956, the Indian Act was amended further to allow members of Indian reserves to contest the legitimacy of children. Under section 12(2), if it was decided that the father of a child was not an Indian, then that child would not be entitled to statutory registration or to band membership: "The addition to a Band List of the name of an illegitimate child ... may be protested at any time within twelve months after the addition, and if upon the protest it is decided that the father of the child was not an Indian, the child is not entitled to be registered."[6] From 1956 on, Indian women's status, at least in the legal sense, meant nothing since only men could bestow legitimacy on their children. This change in policy represented a major encroachment on Indigenous sovereignty, especially for those Indigenous peoples who had, prior to contact, traced kinship matrilineally (Goodleaf 1995; Sunseri 2011). In addition, within Status Indian communities, individual members could adopt a discourse of patrilineage at their discretion. The amendment essentially invited Status Indians to participate in the patriarchal oppression of their own people (Nicholas 1994). After 1951, it became illegal for an Indian woman who married out to live on a reserve in Canada, and male-dominated band councils were expected to enforce the rules. Even when a woman separated from her husband or was widowed, she could not return to live in her reserve community (Silman 1987; Simpson 2014, 16). The social and psychological impact of these laws on the women and children of intermarriages has only been partially documented (Jamieson 1978, 69–72; Silman 1987). In some cases, residency provisions meant that women were separated from their ancestors, friends, and relatives (Weaver 1983). It also meant that their descendants, male and female, were kept from residency on reserves and from playing a part in the governance of reserve-based communities created and determined by Canada's Indian Act (see Jamieson 1986; also Monture-Angus 1999b, 141).

When Indian women were made unequal to Indian men under the Indian Act, they were also made unequal to settler women and their descendants, fostering resentment and divisions between Indigenous women and settler women. For a period of 135 years – from 1850 to 1985 – settler women acquired Indian status upon marriage to registered Indian men.

Clearly, the experience of sexism was not uniform among women in Canada, especially where Indianness is concerned. We know little about how settler women addressed, were conscious of being complicit in, or disagreed with legislative regimes involving Indianness and identity regulation in Canada. However, they were affected by the Indian Act as much as Indigenous women. In many cases, as the wives of Indian men and the mothers of mixed ethnocultural children, they lived and participated in reserve life and politics for generations. After 1951, they also gained band membership, with all of its attendant rights. Although Katherine Ellinghuus (2006) has explored the issue of white women marrying Indigenous men in the United States and Australia, no one has given a voice to their experiences in Canada because of the assumed homogeneity of the status Indian collective. We have little precise knowledge about the racialized politics of Indianness in the Canadian context.

In *Enough Is Enough: Aboriginal Women Speak Out*, Janet Silman addresses how racialized politics played themselves out in some Status Indian communities (also see Simpson 2000). She quotes a woman confronting the competition and hierarchy put in place because of Indian status:

> Something I don't think other people are aware of ... is the hurt that comes with [the Indian Act]. No white woman actually came up and said anything to me personally, but there is one married to a man on this reserve that came up to my friend, [name]. [Name] had got up to say something at a band meeting, and this woman said, "Aw shut up! You non-status don't have nothing to say here." That hurt. (Silman 1987, 219)

These types of divisions are not easily healed. Even today, there remains a certain disquiet among some Status Indians about settler women who acquired Indian status and band membership. The effect of legislation has been to create, and institutionalize, a hierarchical system of relations based on race, status, and rights. Legal distinctions have affected, and still affect today, the material circumstances and entitlements of both Indian and non-Indian women.

THIS EXPLORATION OF the evolution of the Indian Act allows for two conclusions. First, competing interests based on gender cannot be understood without historical context. The creation of gendered hierarchies within Status Indian communities began at contact and were reaffirmed and consolidated by colonial policy and the Indian Act. The Indian Act naturalized Indianness and patrilineal descent through its status provisions, barring Indigenous women from transmitting status and band membership to their children and making them legally subject to their fathers or husbands. Sexism also operated in the Indian Act through the imposition of Eurocentric and patriarchal notions of "illegitimacy" and through discriminatory band membership codes. The ranking of bodies, based along racialized and gender lines, is clearly a manifestation of historical configurations of power.

Racism and sexism were also evident in the imposed elective system of governance. Within this system, governing one's community for Status Indians not only meant following a "superior" system based on the concept of hierarchal authority – it also meant the political exclusion of women. Women were excluded from voting for band elections for more than fifty years, and all-male band councils were invested with the power to disinherit Indian women when they married out. Even when band councils were given the opportunity to determine their own membership in 1985, only 19 percent chose to suspend section 12(1)(b), which had formerly been section 3(c) of the 1876 Indian Act (Lawrence 2004, 61). Although band councils have perpetuated sexism, there were clearly some men who outwardly opposed it. Regardless, the asymmetrical and institutionalized power relations that the Indian Act fostered between Indigenous women and men cannot be denied. Today, these disparate configurations of power are reflected in the disproportionate number of men involved in political decision-making matters at the band, national, and constitutional levels. Conflicts of interest between Indian men and women, whenever they arise, are rooted, at the structural level, in racism and sexism.

The second and more central conclusion is that the racialized injustice of Indianness has been realized through sexism, producing distinct forms of subjugation in the lives of Indian women and their children. When Indian women were made unequal to Indian men under the Indian Act because of sexism, they were also made unequal to settler women and their descendants under an imposed and legislatively sanctioned system of racialization. Indian women have been discriminated against as women, and they have also been discriminated against as Indians. Therefore, Indigenous people must collectively face the sexism imposed on our communities by the Canadian state and the racialized injustice that is Indianness. Given this historical reality, we need to stop thinking about the sexism and Indianness as separate categories or domains of experience and start thinking about them as a system of relations that has structured the politics of recognition and our (re)productive activities.

Sexism, Racialized Injustice, and
Lavell v Canada, 1969–73

A S EARLY AS 1950, Indigenous women began to take exception to the inequality created between men and women through the Indian Act, particularly sections 12(1)(b) and 11(1)(f). For instance, Mary Two Axe Earley, a Kanyen'kéhaka woman from Kahnawà:ke spoke out against the patriarchy and sexism inherent within the legal presumption that women would follow the status of their husbands upon marriage. During the 1950s and '60s, however, these women's protests garnered little widespread support because there were few political venues in which to articulate them. The feminist movement changed things. Two Axe Earley submitted a brief to the Royal Commission on the Status of Women in Canada, and its final report "recommended that the Indian Act be amended to allow an Indian woman upon marriage to a non-Indian to a) retain her Indian status and b) transmit her Indian status to her children" (Canada 1970, 238; also see Borrows 1994). Despite the step forward, Two Axe Earley would have to wait until the mid-1980s before any changes were made to the Indian Act, which continued to wreak havoc on Indian communities.

Indigenous women's political aspirations in Canada had two goals: to restore women's birthright so that they and their children could rejoin the Status Indian collective as legally disenfranchised peoples (that is, to have the sexual equality of Indigenous women recognized under colonial legislation) and to combat Western sexism and heteropatriarchy (that is, to challenge and subvert the concept of Indianness). In other words, Indigenous women did not put forth their grievances as either Indians or women – they acted as Indian women. They spoke out about the intolerance and discrimination they were suffering at the hands of both the Canadian and Status Indian governments, and they challenged the injustices and misdirected hostilities that were overtaking Status Indian communities. The lack of attention they received from the Canadian government following the royal commission led a few women to seek justice through the courts. By attempting to end discrimination through the equality provisions of the Canadian Bill of Rights, which had been passed in 1960, they sought judicial, as opposed to legislative, reform.

JEANNETTE LAVELL (NÉE CORBIERE) was the first woman in Canada to bring forth litigation aimed at challenging section 12(1)(b) of the Indian Act. An Anishinaabe-kwe from Wiikwemkoong Unceded Indian Reserve, located in what is currently called Manitoulin Island, Lavell became a non-Indian when she married David Lavell in the 1960s. When she received confirmation from Canada's Indian registrar that she could not have her children registered as Indians, she brought her case before a county court in 1971. The court dismissed her case, though it did leave room for an appeal. Justice Groberman reasoned that "if section 12(1)(b) is distasteful or undesirable to Indians, they themselves can arouse public conscience and thereby stimulate Parliament by legislative amendment to correct any unfairness or injustice."[1] When her case was heard in the Federal Court of Appeal in October 1971, her status was restored, and Canada – aroused by the implications of the decision, one that stood to increase the number of Status Indians – vowed to bring the case before the Supreme Court for further clarification (Weaver 1993). The case was not heard until February 1974, and it was heard alongside that of Yvonne Bédard, a woman in similar circumstances.[2]

Bédard, a Haudenosaunee woman from my own community, the Six Nations at Grand River Territory, had likewise lost her status when she married a non-Indian. Upon divorcing her husband, she and her children returned to the reserve to live in a home willed to her by her mother (Weaver 1974). Through appeals to the band council, Bédard received permission to reside on the reserve for one year, after which time she was required to dispose of all property in accordance with the Indian Act. After being granted an extension on her permit for residency, she was threatened with a band council eviction notice. Bédard sought legal counsel and – based on the *Lavell* precedent – won her case in the Ontario Supreme Court in 1973. What came to be known as the *Lavell-Bédard* case reached the Supreme Court of Canada in February 1974. In a five to four decision, the two litigants each lost their case.

Mary Two Axe Earley, Jeannette Lavell, Yvonne Bédard, and countless other unnamed women sought to restore to Indigenous women rights that had been denied to them since the imposition of the Indian Act. Lavell and Bédard were, in effect, challenging the expectation that they would assume the race of their husbands – either Indian or non-Indian – because of their gender as women. In challenging a system of interlocking discrimination that had historically made them unequal to settler women and Indian men, their litigation was intended to restore rights and privileges that settler colonialism and dominance had sought to undo. A Maliseet woman from the Tobique Reservation in New Brunswick shed light on the sheer complexity of grievances being put forward by women of the day:

We all knew that no government agency – be it white or be it Indian – was going to tell us we were no longer Indian, when we *know* we are Indian. Here the Canadian government was making instant Indians out of white women. You might as well say they were trying to make instant white women out of us Indians. And it cannot be, because being Indian is our heritage: it's in our blood. I think that is our determination right there – it's because we are Indian. We were fighting for our birthright. (Silman 1987, 9)

These women sought to challenge patriarchal structures that empowered men through the status, citizenship, inheritance, and governance sections of the Indian Act. They were seeking a resolution to a centuries-long series of laws that had treated them unfairly in relation to Indian men and settler women. Neither Jeannette Lavell nor Yvonne Bédard received much support from band councils, Status Indians, or Status Indian organizations such as the National Indian Brotherhood, now the Assembly of First Nations.

THEIR CASES FOLLOWED centuries of government interference in federally recognized communities, interference that had resulted in social changes, lands appropriation, and dispossession. In Kahnawà:ke, the homeland of Mary Two Axe Earley, near what is still today Tio'tia:ke (where the currents meet, or Montreal), the federal government had sanctioned the seizure and theft of the St. Lawrence Seaway (Simpson 2014, 50–53). Acts of dispossession are a familiar story to many Indigenous nations, including the Haudenosaunee. Like Kahnawà:ke, my own nation faced a series of land expropriations at the hands of settlers and the Canadian state. Under the Haldimand Proclamation, we were allotted 950,000 acres of land on October 25, 1784 – an indemnification for territory lost in what is now New York State during the War of

Independence (S. Hill 2017, 143, 146; C. Johnston 1964, 128; R. Monture 2014, 1; Six Nations Lands and Resources 2008). The land was partitioned into six blocks within which each of the Six Nations set out national boundaries and determined their clan lands (Doxtator 1996, 220; see also S. Hill 2017, 140–42). The clan system was the basis upon which land was distributed, and each nation likely organized itself around women, since they were the key to kinship organization (also see Doxtator 1996, 220–21).

The original grant of over a half-million acres did not remain in the possession of the Six Nations for long. Some 350,000 acres were sold to settlers between 1784 and 1798 (C. Johnston 1964, lv). Many of these sales were conducted by Joseph Brant, a Mohawk chief, though it is not clear what his motives might have been, although some have speculated (S. Hill 2017, 155–62; R. Monture 2014, 29–61; C. Johnston 1964). Following the sales, Euro-Canadians continued to settle along the Grand River, and at least four other major land surrenders were made in the 1830s to accommodate the influx (C. Johnston 1994, 178). There were additional land losses, but not all of them were authorized surrenders. Indeed, unauthorized squatting was common on Haudenosaunee lands (C. Johnston 1994; also see S. Hill 2017, 168–69), and a scattering of Six Nations members conducted unauthorized dealings beyond the control of chiefs and other officials who were responsible for land disbursements (Doxtator 1996, 225). Formal transactions generated revenue, including an $800,000 band fund in the mid-1800s (S. Hill 2017, 178–80; Weaver 1994, 182). The government later invested a portion of these funds, "without the knowledge of any responsible spokespersons for the Confederacy," in the ill-fated Grand River Navigation Company (S. Hill 2017, 178–80; C. Johnston 1994, 178). And no amount of money could restore the 350,000 acres lost in the late eighteenth century. By 1847, the land base at Grand River had been reduced to a mere 55,000 acres, less than 16 percent of the original allotment.

The reduction of the size of the original Haldimand tract placed significant pressures on the land. In 1785, the Six Nations comprised 1,843 members who occupied 950,000 acres of land; in 1847, 2,200 members occupied 55,000 acres (Doxator 1996). In short, squatters, settlers, and leasees encroached on the Grand River Haudenosaunee, ushering in years of political upheaval, particularly in the1830s. In 1841, "fearful that all of their land would be lost to settlers," the *royaner* (hereditary chiefs) of the Confederacy asked the British government to remove all Euro-Canadians from Six Nations land, but they were unsuccessful (Doxator 1996, 225). Six years later, in 1847, the Haudenosaunee moved to a consolidated reserve territory in the Township of Tuscarora, where they continue to reside today. The move resulted in a number of social and political losses for Grand River Haudenosaunee. It placed pressure on the Six Nations to conform to European social, political, and economic structures, including the adoption of individual land allotments (Doxator 1996, 228). The allotment system stood in direct contrast to the system of national clan territories, and it required an adjustment of the customary matrilineal system.

In practical and pragmatic ways, the decision to implement the system was influenced by settler encroachments on their land. Put simply, the hereditary chiefs needed some way to preclude *ha dih nyoh* (white settler) men from gaining further access to Haudenosaunee lands. In fact, they were concerned about Haudenosaunee women marrying settler men – unions that would automatically entitle the men (and any children of the marriage) to a stake in the community and its lands, which could then be leased, sold, or surrendered against the council's wishes, impacting the community's overall prosperity. Thus, the decision to switch to a form of kinship organization that centred on the father rather the mother worked in the interest of protecting Six Nations lands. Indeed, and as Mohawk scholar Deborah Doxtator (1996, 248) writes:

> The Six Nations council regulations that members be related by birth or marriage to a Six Nations man meant that outside men would be excluded from owning and possibly trying to sell land from the reserve. The Six Nations had experienced early losses of reserve lands given to Euro-Canadian husbands. These men invariably appealed to the British colonial government to be able to exercise their property rights under British law.

Ha dih nyoh men gaining community membership and an entitlement to land was a disturbing but ever-present reality at nineteenth-century Grand River. The allotment system effectively blocked ha dih nyoh men from owning land or from appealing to a colonial government that had become increasingly hostile to Haudenosaunee concerns. The adoption of a patriarchal approach to governance and politics was in fact a pragmatic and quite sensible response to the infiltration of European ideas and land encroachments.

In other words, by the mid-twentieth century, Grand River Haudenosaunee – like many other Indigenous and Status Indian communities in Canada – had become accustomed to a system of land theft and encroachments. We became familiar with settler populations who, as Mohawk scholar Susan Hill (2017, 168) has written, "never even bothered to secure a fraudulent purchase from any Haudenosaunee individual – they simply came upon a piece of land, looked around to see if any other white man was there and, if finding none, took possession of it." These developments changed the way Indigenous people perceived themselves and the people around them. We became peoples, as Audra Simpson (2014, 53) writes, "with shared past and present interests, who were radically different from those around them, and who could now be intruded upon, in what were perceived to be terrible ways, without consent, with indifference and with the law." The opposition directed at women such as Jeanette Lavell and Yvonne Bédard, herself from Six Nations, looks different in this context. On the one hand, these women sought to overturn injustices brought on by Canada and to rejoin the Status Indian collective – they were warriors in their own right. On the other hand, from the perspective of their own communities, who were now discriminating against them and even banishing them altogether, they were a symbol of all that needed to be protected in Indian country, notably, a "takeover by non-Indian men" (Simpson 2014, 60). At Grand River Territory, as elsewhere across the country, patriarchy became one of several adaptations to a "colonial scene." As Simpson argues, "extinguishing the rights of Mohawk women may have been less an attempt at discriminating against their own people than at protecting the community from a possible takeover by non-Indian men" (60).

OPPOSITION AGAINST WOMEN such as Lavell and Bédard was also shaped by the political climate of the 1970s. The most vocal opponents expressed fear that Status Indians would lose special citizenship rights if Canada's Bill of Rights – the human rights legislation governing Canada before the Canadian Charter of Rights and Freedoms came into effect in 1982 – came to supersede the Indian Act (Cardinal 1977).[3] Status Indian organizations believed this could come to pass if the courts deemed all sections – not just section 12(1)(b) – to be in violation of the equality provisions of the Bill of Rights (Weaver 1993). This fear, which largely overshadowed the Lavell and Bédard cases and the political lobbying efforts of Indigenous women, was brought to the fore by Canada's White Paper.

In 1969, Prime Minister Pierre Trudeau and Jean Chrétien, the minister of Indian Affairs and Northern Development, introduced a policy paper titled "Statement of the Government of Canada on Indian Policy, 1969" (Canada 1969; also Turner 2006). This apparently "new" policy was couched in the language of liberalism and promised to provide Indians with the same rights afforded to settler populations. The Indian Act would be repealed, restoring to Indians "the right to full and equal participation in the cultural, social, political and economic milieu of Canada" (Canada 1969, 6). The paper proposed to abolish Indian status – not in the sense of repairing the colonial injustice known as Indianness but rather in the sense that Indians would be offered "the same citizenship status and rights as non-Indians and nothing more" (Satzewich and Wotherspoon 1993, 230). They would secure provincial services through the same channels as other citizens. In short, the White Paper sought to devolve legislative responsibility for Indians from the federal government to the provinces (Turner 2006; Weaver 1981).

The White Paper met with unparalleled opposition in many Status Indian communities. Status Indians identified the document as yet another assimilationist policy intended to terminate our relationship with Canada as citizens of Indigenous nations. The White Paper would remove rights protected by the Indian Act, and these rights were felt to be significant insofar as they "differed from those in the treaties, land claim settlements and Canadian constitution" (Weaver 1993, 99; also see Coates 2008). The act ensured federal responsibility for such things as education, health care, social services, and a land base (held in perpetuity). The general sentiment towards the White Paper was captured in a statement issued by the National Indian Brotherhood:

> The policy proposals put forward by the Minister of Indian Affairs are not acceptable to the Indian people of Canada ... We view this as a policy designed to divest us of our aboriginal, *residual and statutory rights*. If we accept this

policy, and in the process lose our rights and our lands, we become willing partners in cultural genocide. This we cannot do. (Frideres 1983, 104; emphasis mine)

Harold Cardinal, president of the Indian Association of Alberta, put it in different words:

> The new Indian policy ... presented in June of 1969 is a thinly disguised programme of extermination through assimilation. For the Indian to survive, says the government, in effect, he must become a good little brown white man. The Americans to the south of us used to have a saying: "The only good Indian is a dead Indian." The Macdonald-Chrétien doctrine would amend this but slightly to, "The only good Indian is a non-Indian." (Cardinal 1969, 1)

From east to west, the White Paper was clearly and emphatically denounced by Status Indian and treaty organizations. Canada withdrew the policy but, arguably, it has not reversed the policy's assimilative bent (see Turner 2006, 2013; also see J.R. Miller 1989).

In this context, Indian organizations became increasingly preoccupied with the special and distinct rights of Status Indians. They defended the Indian Act and opposed cases such as *Lavell-Bédard* that threatened it. In 1972, the National Indian Brotherhood decided at a conference – and in the notable absence of unanimous support – to formally intervene in the case (Cheda 1977, 205). Regena Crowchild and Harold Cardinal explained to a House of Commons Standing Committee on Indian Affairs and Northern Development that

> we all, both male and female, realize the jeopardy this case has placed us in, and as a people condemn it and all of its possible implications ... If the *Canadian Bill of Rights* is

given precedence over the Indian Act, it will thus effectively render the Indian Act inoperative in its most important areas and endanger the definition and the protection of the Status Indian.[4]

Some individuals and leaders made arguments in favour of sex discrimination. Speaking on behalf of a once matrilineal nation of people, the Association of Iroquois and Allied Indians proclaimed: "It is the legal and moral duty of the husband to support his wife. Consequently, by the Indian Act, the woman lost her Indian status and took the status of the husband. This section in the Indian Act was merely a legislative embodiment of what had become Indian custom" (Weaver 1993, 98; see also Sanders 1975, 671). Others dismissed Lavell's and Bédard's efforts as the result of feminist influence (Krosenbrink-Gelissen 1991; *Ottawa Journal* 1971; Sanders 1975; Weaver 1993). Others argued that, in marrying non-Indians, women had to be prepared to suffer the consequences of disenfranchisement (see Cardinal 1977, 111).

At times, people overlooked the fact that the enfranchisement of these women had been involuntarily and that it had been a part of Indigenous peoples' racialization as Indians since the 1850s. In a letter to the editor of the *Brantford Expositor*, published as "Viewpoint of an Indian" on September 14, 1971, one person reflected on the plight of Yvonne Bédard as follows: "The situation of Mrs Bédard is defined in the Act. I am in agreement with the elective council's decision on this case and I commend the council for its compliance with the regulations in the Act. Mrs Bédard should remember the old adage: 'You have made your bed – now lie in it.'" These public statements and debates were a disturbing but altogether familiar manifestation of the extent to which the history of colonial dominance and racialization has come to alter and devastate Indigenous peoples' relationship with Canada and with one another. The fear that Canada would terminate its relationship with Indigenous nations under the guise of benevolently revoking the category "Indian" needs to be seen for what it was: a strategy on behalf of the settler state to reinscribe the colonial dominance that is none other than Indianness in Canada. This strategy was but one instance in a long-standing refusal on the part of Canada to recognize its nation-to-nation relationship with Indigenous peoples.

The White Paper was intended to draw us further into a political relationship and dialogue we have had with Canada as Indians. As proposed legislation, it followed in the footsteps of a long line of Indian policy that sought to expropriate lands and to establish, define, regulate, reduce, and then ultimately extinguish the registered Indian population. The White Paper might well be considered what Mohawk scholar Gerald Taiaike Alfred refers to as "assimilation's end-game." As Alfred (2005, 126) rightly suggests, its goal was

> the terminological and psychic displacement of authentic indigenous identities, beliefs, and behaviours with one designed by Indian Department bureaucrats, government lawyers, and judges to complete the imperial objective of exterminating Onkwehonwe presences from the social and political landscape. It [sought] the annihilation of an independent existence for the original peoples, a cultural and political-economic process of state-sponsored identity invention to dispossess and assimilate the remnants of the Onkwehonwe who are still tied to this land and to indigenous ways of life.

The Canadian government did nothing to revisit the colonial policies that had produced the category "Indian" in the first place, including the process whereby it first emerged as an ordinary or taken-for-granted way of conducting politics; Canada did nothing to address, disrupt, or otherwise reconcile the expectation and requirement that Indigenous nations would appropriate and work within the confines of Indianness. Nor did it address the fact that Indianness was preferable to Canada where administrative, fiduciary, and political dealings are concerned. As if it had amnesia, Canada proposed to remove the category it had itself imposed in order to define and then regulate us as racialized people. Canada was clearly unwilling to acknowledge or take into consideration the sociolegal contexts that had prevented Indigenous nations from being recognized as sovereign peoples. Indeed, awareness and recognition of the sociolegal and political developments that had suppressed our own nationhood-based approaches to identity and citizenship – and, more importantly, the legal processes that might go about restoring our sovereign jurisdiction over these matters – were not part of the politics of the day.

Indianness – that is to say race – mattered in the 1970s but not in the sense of any critical or embodied engagement with the category "Indian." Race mattered, as Simpson (2014, 59) notes, because we had become Indians, and "being Indian carried rights." Through the White Paper, which proposed to benevolently turn us into ordinary citizens of Canada (Thobani 2007, 51–52), we would experience a politics aimed at our legislative extinguishment and elimination as peoples (Wolfe 2006).

Given that the government had framed its new policy in the language of liberalism, Indigenous organizations had only a few avenues at their disposal to address the shortcomings of the White Paper. As Anishinaabe scholar Dale Turner (2006, 29–36) has argued, these limitations resulted from the failure of liberal policy makers to address the legacy of colonialism, to see Indigenous rights as *sui generis* (in a class of their own) and not as minority rights, to question the legitimacy of Canadian state formation and, finally, to include Indigenous peoples in a workable theory of rights and participation. I would add further that there was a failure on behalf of Canada – and, indeed, at times, Status Indian organizations – to connect histories of racialized injustice with sexism. That Status Indian organizations intervened in *Lavell-Bédard* attests to the degree to which an inability to see racism and sexism as concomitant systems of power had come to define, determine, and dominate Status Indian politics. The most serious – though possibly inadvertent – misconception was thinking of the history of settler colonialism in either/or terms. Status Indians were influenced (and at times encouraged) by Parliament, the courts, and even Indian organizations to participate in a way of thinking that detached the history of racialization from that of sexism. At the time, this either/or thinking could not be reconciled, largely because the White Paper was not seen as part of the same history of sexism that had sought to extinguish Indigenous peoples through their racialization as Indians.

THE DEGREE TO WHICH either/or thinking dominated Indian policy is evident when *Lavell-Bédard* is considered alongside *Drybones*, a case that also centred on the Bill of Rights.[5] In 1970, Joseph Drybones, a citizen of the Dene Nation from what is now called Yellowknife, Northwest Territories, petitioned the Supreme Court of Canada to have section 95(b) of the Indian Act declared unconstitutional on the grounds that it violated section 1(b) of the Canadian Bill of Rights. Drybones had been apprehended in a Yellowknife tavern, the Olde Stope Hotel, because he had been drinking alcohol. Section 95(b) read: "An Indian who ... is intoxicated ... off a reserve, is guilty of an offence and is liable on summary conviction to a fine not less than ten dollars and not more than fifty dollars or to imprisonment for a term not exceeding three months or to both fine and imprisonment."[6] His lawyers argued that because the law treated Indians more harshly for being intoxicated in public than it did non-Indians, it violated section 1(b) of the Bill of Rights, which guaranteed all Canadians – including Indians – equality "without discrimination by reason of race, national origin, colour, religion or sex" and also "the right of the individual to equality before the law and the protection of the law." They argued, successfully, that the Indian Act violated Drybones's guarantee of "equality before the law irrespective of race, colour, or national origin" (Morton 1992, 399).

Indigenous women viewed the ruling as a positive development, especially since they were arguing that section 12(1)(b) of the Indian Act discriminated against them by virtue of sex. Kathleen Jamieson (1978) later commented that they thought that section 12(1)(b) might be declared discriminatory in a compound sense, because it placed Indigenous women into an unequal relationship with Indigenous men on account of their gender, and because it placed Indigenous women into an unequal relation with non-Indigenous women on account of their race or Indianness. The idea was to call attention to matters of Indianness – indeed, race – and to the fact that Indian status is based on one's (grand)parents' gender. They argued, as I do, that people became non-Indians because of their gender and also because of the racialized way of thinking that had constructed the category "Indian."

The Supreme Court came to an entirely different conclusion when it heard the case in 1974. In a majority decision, the court held that the Canadian Bill of Rights could not overrule the Indian Act as a piece of federal legislation. Justice Ritchie reasoned: "The Bill of Rights is not effective to render inoperative legislation, such as S. 12(1)(b) of the *Indian Act*, passed by the Parliament of Canada in discharge of its constitutional function under S. 91(24) of the *B.N.A. Act*, to specify how and by whom Crown lands reserved for Indians are to be used."[7] The court effectively exonerated Canada from a history of discrimination based on racism and sexism.

Canada was immune from having the question of discrimination come under the scrutiny of its own antidiscrimination laws because it had unilaterally granted itself the authority to claim jurisdiction over what it called "Indians" under the Constitution Act, 1867.

The court also bypassed the claims of Indigenous women by interpreting *equality before the law* narrowly. Justice Ritchie stated: "The question is confined to deciding whether Parliament, in defining Indian status so as to exclude women of Indian birth who have married non-Indians, enacted a law which cannot be sensibly construed without abrogating, abridging or infringing the rights of such women to equality before the law."[8] He continued:

> "Equality before the Law" ... carries the meaning of equal subjection of all classes to the ordinary courts, and in my opinion the phrase "equally before the law" as employed in section 1(b) of the Bill of Rights is to be treated as meaning equality in the administration of the law by the law enforcement authorities and the ordinary courts of the land.[9]

As Justice Ritchie reasoned, the issue before the court was not whether there was (in)equality in the substance of the law but whether there was (in)equality in its administration. The court argued that since all Indian women lost status when they married non-Indians or unregistered persons, all Indigenous women were being guaranteed equality of protection in the law's administration.

The definition of equality before the law granted by the court stunned legal scholars (see Monture-Angus 1995, 134–37) because it contradicted the earlier *Drybones* decision. In fact, Justice Laskin made this precise argument in his dissenting judgment:

If, as in *Drybones,* discrimination by reason of race makes certain statutory provisions inoperative, the same result must follow as to statutory provisions which exhibit discrimination by reason of sex ... If for the words "on account of race" there are substituted the words "on account of sex" the result must surely be the same where a Federal enactment imposes disabilities or prescribes disqualifications for members of the female sex which are not imposed upon members of the male sex in the same circumstances.[10]

Despite Laskin's reasoning, he was unable to persuade the court to reconsider its final judgment. In fact, Justice Ritchie countered that there was a fundamental distinction to be drawn between the *Lavell-Bédard* and *Drybones* cases – a distinction that Justice Laskin had overlooked:

[It] ... appears to me to be that the impugned section in the latter case could not be enforced without denying equality of treatment in the administration and enforcement of the law before the ordinary courts of the land to a racial group, whereas no such inequality of treatment between Indian men and women flows as a necessary result of the application of s. 12(1)(b) of the Indian Act.[11]

This distinction was regarded as peculiar by some legal scholars. For example, Walter Tarnopolsky (1975, 160) commented:

Surely such a fundamental distinction requires some justification ... [for] how can it be denied that Indian women who marry non-Indians are not equally treated before the ordinary courts of the land, when in the administration and enforcement of the law the courts must deny them property rights, status and access to their native territory, because of a provision which applies to them and not to

Indian men? Surely this is a greater inequality before the law, more fundamental and more drastic, than the relatively minor inequality dealt with in the *Drybones* case?

This is perhaps one of the most puzzling aspects of the Supreme Court judgment, but it appears that Justice Ritchie reasoned that Indian women had the freedom to choose not to lose legal status at marriage (Jamieson 1978, 85); they could avoid the application or effects of section 12(1)(b) by simply rejecting settlers (or unregistered Indians) as partners. The court seemed to be suggesting that Indian women willingly chose institutionalized discrimination when they intermarried. It suggested that – on a daily basis – there is a *choice* between being a woman or an Indian, even though Indigenous women had argued that this is clearly not the case (see Monture-Angus 1995, 136–37). By employing a narrow interpretation of equality before the law, the court ruled that discrimination must be proven and necessarily present within the law's administration, not in the substance of the law. *Equality before the law* did not mean that individuals had equal rights before the law, only that all people were equally bound by the law's administration and enforcement. By this definition, Jeanette Lavell and Yvonne Bédard had been treated equally before the law in the eyes of the Supreme Court.

WHAT THE COURT DIDN'T consider was the issue of race. At the outset of the judgment, Justice Ritchie commented, "The contention which formed the basis of the argument submitted by both respondents was that they had been denied equality before the law by reason of sex, and I propose to deal with the matter on this basis."[12] That the court focused only on sex discrimination was not a problem in and of itself. Rather, the court failed to explicitly delimit the boundaries of sex discrimination – that is, it did not specify with whom they were comparing Indigenous women's experiences. After all, the court had defined the issue as equality in the administration – not the substance – of the law. The court did not, in other words, entertain the notion of substantive inequality – that treating people the same may further produce and entrench inequality (see Baines 2006, 73).

To arrive at its decision, the court overlooked numerous historical facts and skirted recognizing that sex discrimination is always interlocked with race discrimination, that the Indian Act made racialized distinctions, some of them compulsory, between all women in Canada through sections 12(1)(b) and 11(1)(f) (see Maracle 1993, 124). Instead, when the court addressed the issue of sex discrimination, it narrowed the scope of the inquiry to comparing the treatment of Indian women who had married out to Status Indian men. In essence, had the court looked at the administration of the law in reference to all women, it would have had to recognize that settler women of non-Indigenous birth were gaining status under section 11(1)(f). In short, what the court needed to do in *Lavell-Bédard* (in order to secure justice for Indigenous women and their male children) was to broaden the scope of antidiscrimination law to include all women legally defined and racialized as Indians. It did not. The consequence of that decision was to focus on sex discrimination as something fundamentally unrelated to Indianness.

By disregarding the possibility that section 12(1)(b) brought about unequal treatment in the administration and enforcement of the law to a racial group, the court dismissed the way in which the Indian Act operated simultaneously as a racist and patriarchal piece of legislation. It was as if Jeanette Lavell and Yvonne Bédard were not Indians at all, let alone litigating against the inequality facing their male and female children – and indeed all Status Indians. The court furthered the ongoing and symbolic removal of Indian women from the Status Indian collective, reaffirming for

Indian women and their children their status as legislated outsiders. In essence, a one-dimensional way of thinking about discrimination in the law in turn concealed the systemic nature of Indigenous women's discrimination. The assertion that all Indian women experienced sex discrimination in the same way in Canada needs to be seen for what it was – an act of colonial power and a refusal by the judiciary on behalf of Canada to address matters of race and how all women, on account of race and gender, were placed into unequal standing with one another. *Lavell-Bédard* at once recovered and recuperated settler colonialism and affirmed settler sovereignty.

The court's failure to acknowledge the process whereby Indigenous people became Indians through a legislative history of sexism and racialization reflects the limited scope of anti-discrimination law in Canada, certainly with respect to Indigenous peoples (see Baines 1993; Crenshaw 1989; Razack 1999). The court had an opportunity to acknowledge and reconcile the matter of racialized injustice as it is realized through, and inseparable from, sexism, but it failed in the end to embrace the link between the two as systems, of discrimination. In fact, the court concluded there was no discrimination at all. The decision did little to rectify the injustice done to Indigenous women and simply pushed the historical relationship between racism and patriarchy to the margins.

To better comprehend the stance of Status Indian communities on the *Lavell-Bédard* case, we need to understand that their failure to acknowledge the interconnectedness of racialization and sexism was, in part, the result of these interlocking systems and their promotion of divided loyalties and competing interests. By the 1970s, Indianness and patriarchy had come to be so internalized and institutionalized that Status Indians felt that their very existence and survival depended on them. The adoption of patriarchy at both the community and national level of politics had also become a pragmatic and quite sensible way to subvert European ideas and encroachments on Indigenous lands. In this context, women who married out were viewed by Status Indians as the legislated outsiders they had become.

Individual versus Collective Rights in Status Indian Politics, 1985–99

C ANADA DID NOT AMEND the Indian Act until 1985, when Bill C-31 became law. The change was finally prompted by the enactment of the Canadian Charter of Rights and Freedoms in 1982. After 1982, section 12(1)(b) of the Indian Act – if left intact – would have violated section 15 of the Charter, which stated: "Every individual is equal before and under the law and has the right to equal benefit of the law without discrimination and, in particular, without discrimination based on race, national or ethnic origin, colour, religion, sex, age, or mental and physical disability."

Activism by front-line women's organizations (see Silman 1987) and litigation by women such as Mary Two Axe Earley and Jeanette Lavell also played a role, particularly following the near condemnation of Canada's human rights reputation brought on by the *Sandra Lovelace v Canada* decision in 1981. In December 1977, Lovelace, a citizen of the Wolastoqiyik (Maliseet) Nation and now a Canadian senator and recipient of the Order of Canada, had complained to the United Nations about the Indian Act, claiming that it contravened article 27 of the International Covenant on Civil and Political Liberties, which reads: "In those States in which ethnic, religious or linguistic minorities exist, persons belonging to such minorities shall not be denied the right, in community with the other members of their group, to enjoy their own culture, to profess and practise their own religion, or to use their own language."[1] The UN Human Rights Committee ruled in favour of Lovelace on July 30, 1981. Canada was held in violation of a covenant it had signed in the 1960s. The UN did not, however, condemn the historical practice of excluding women because of sex discrimination in the operation of section 12(1)(b) of the Indian Act. Rather, it found that Canada had violated an international treaty by enacting a law that had kept Lovelace from her culture. In the words of the committee:

> The case of Sandra Lovelace should be considered in the light of the fact that her marriage to a non-Indian has broken up. It is natural that in such a situation she wishes to return to the environment in which she was born, particularly as after the dissolution of her marriage her main cultural attachment again was to the Maliseet band. Whatever may be the merits of the *Indian Act* in other respects, it does not seem to the Committee that to deny Sandra Lovelace the right to reside on the reserve is reasonable, or necessary to preserve the identity of the tribe. The Committee therefore concludes that to prevent her recognition as belonging to the band is an unjustifiable denial of her rights under article 27 of the Covenant, read in the context of the other provisions referred to.[2]

Although the UN lacked the power to change Canadian law, the case was viewed as a victory for Indigenous women.

When Bill C-31 became law on June 28, 1985, it was intended to accomplish three objectives: it would terminate the infamous section 12(1)(b) that Sandra Lovelace and so many other women had protested, it would return status to those who had lost it, and it would increase the power of band councils or Indian Act governments to determine band membership. Both sections 12(1)(b) and 11(1)(f) were terminated, and people, including women and their children who had been involuntarily enfranchised, started to register as Indians under one of seven different sections of the Indian Act, including sections 6(1) and 6(2), which outlined who could and could not pass status to their children and led to the infamous two-generation cut off.

THE PASSAGE OF C-31 into law raised a storm of controversy. As Cree scholar Verna Kirkness (1987–88, 415) wrote at the time, "Discrimination against women has not been removed from the Indian Act: it has merely been partially suspended for two generations." Nor did the amendments eradicate asymmetrical power relations established through governance and racialized ways of thinking and knowing. The changes did nothing to upset Indian–non-Indian distinctions rooted in earlier versions of the Indian Act. Ha dih nyoh scholar Joan Holmes (1987, 16) commented: "A new law does not erase years of [women's] alienation from their families and communities, deep-seated feelings of rejection and inadequacy, and the struggle to raise their children in a foreign environment." The Indian Act might have put an end to our involuntary enfranchisement as Indians, but it recast sex discrimination in new forms and created newer and more substantive types of inequality.

The 1985 amendments included a number of broad "discriminatory leftovers" (Cannon 1995, 2006) that sparked new human rights grievances and court cases. Among them was a general refusal to address the category Indian. Although many referred to – and indeed continue to refer to – the 1985 amendments as "Bill C-31," the amendments did nothing to remove or reconcile the history of racialization that we have experienced as Indigenous peoples (see Moss 1990, 283). Patricia Monture-Angus (1999a, 71), a Kanyen'kéhaka scholar, commented:

> I think the next time that somebody tells me that they are a Bill C-31 "Indian" I am going to scream. There is no such thing as a Bill C-31 Indian. Once a bill passes into law it is not a bill anymore (maybe this is just a little quirk I have as a result of my legal education). Everyone running around calling themselves Bill C-31 Indians are saying (technically and legally) I am something that does not exist. If we have to be "Indians" then let's all just be "Indians." I would prefer if we could be Mohawk, or Cree, or Tlingit, or Mi'kmaq or Saulteaux. That is who we are (albeit not all expressed in our language). That is the truth. It is important to reclaim who we are at least in our thoughts.

The 1985 Indian Act left intact the discrimination we have been asked to participate in since 1850 – as Indians, as Indian women, and as the children of Indian women who married non-Indians. It simply stigmatized new classes of Indians, who were deemed less than "original" Indians because our (grand)mothers had to be restored to Indian status. As Audra Simpson (2014, 61) notes, people who have their status reinstated are now known as "C-31s" and, for many, "Bill C-31" has become a "categorical identity." That Canada failed to provide resources and land to accommodate "C-31s" as "new members" has only compounded tensions and divisions in Status Indian communities.

While communities could now distinguish between original Status Indians and C-31s, the amendments also led to distinctions between section 6(1) Indians, who could pass status on to their children, and 6(2) Indians, who, as the children of involuntarily enfranchised women, could not pass status on to their own children unless they married a registered Indian. Sharon McIvor, a citizen of the Nlaka'pamux Nation who would go on to challenge the discriminatory nature of the 1985 Indian Act, applied within months of the amendments to be registered as an Indian along with her children. Both of McIvor's grandmothers were Status Indians, but her grandfathers were not. She found out that she could be registered, but that her children could not. In essence, the amendments had simply put off the gender discrimination of the Indian Act by a generation. McIvor launched a court case in 1989, but it wasn't heard until 2007.

As McIvor's case reveals, the Indian Act continued to emphasize a patrilineal method of descent reckoning. In order for children to be registered as Status Indians, an application had to be made to the Registrar, Department of Indian Affairs and Northern Development, and the paternity of the children had to be stated. The Registrar then determined if the parents were married and what subsection of the act they had been registered under as Indians. Both parents' signatures were mandatory. If the parents were unmarried, the father signed a form declaring paternity in order to determine his own registration before the child's status could be decided. If a woman chose not to name the father, if the father was unknown, or if the father was unable to provide the necessary documentation or did not want to take responsibility for the child, the child was registered as having only one Indian parent – the mother. It was assumed that a father was non-Indian if the registration of a male Indian father could not be established at the time of the child's registration. It did not matter that a woman might withhold the name of a father because of rape, incest, sexual assault, or other circumstances that would make it unwise or undesirable to state or name the person (see Eberts 2010, 42–43; M. Mann 2005). It did not matter that paternity stood in significant contrast to the matrilineal system of kinship reckoning that is well documented in many Indigenous nations (see Thomas and Boyle

1994, 149; see also Noon 1949, 36–37). These rules caused a number of children to be registered improperly under section 6(2) or not registered at all (Clatworthy 2003a; Eberts 2010; M. Mann 2005). By making the statement of paternity compulsory, the Indian Act maintained an unequal, and distinctly patriarchal, relationship between male and female Indians. The matter of unstated paternity once again helped define and then reduce the Status Indian population.

The final discriminatory leftover stemmed from the new bylaw-making powers given to individual Indian bands. Although the amendments are said to have "restored" the right of band governments to determine their own members, they actually invited them to create band membership codes that opened the door to more discrimination. Section 10(1) read:

> A band may assume control of its own membership if it establishes membership rules for itself in writing in accordance with this section and if, after the band has given appropriate notice of its intention to assume control of its own membership, a majority of the electors of the band gives its consent to the band's control of its own membership.[3]

Until the 1980s, control of band membership matters rested with the Registrar, and most band members were either Status Indians or individuals admitted to "a general list" (Magnet 2003, 57). After 1985, bands were able to make choices about the persons with whom they wanted to associate or whom they wanted to exclude. They were able to more effectively define the Indian collective. The amendments separated Indian status from band membership (Eberts 2010, 26).

Not every band chose to take control of its own membership. And within the Six Nations at Grand River Territory, a 50 percent majority of people refused to participate in the process of developing a membership code, which led to the minority later developing a residency bylaw that stated that only band members could reside on the reserve (Cannon 2005, 376). In cases where bands chose not to take control, under section 9(1), control remained with the Registrar. By the end of the 1990s, the Registrar had come to control around 60 percent of band membership codes in Canada, while approximately 40 percent of Status Indian bands assumed control over their own membership (see Furi and Wherrett 2003, 10; Magnet 2003, 59). The following four principles of descent-reckoning were written into these codes:

1 One parent rule: used by 90 bands across the country; individuals are eligible for membership if one parent is a band member;
2 Two parent rule: used by 67 bands, individuals are eligible for membership if both parents are band members;
3 Ss. 6(1) and 6(2) of the Indian Act rule: used by 49 bands; also used by bands without a membership code, except that in the latter case the Department of Indian Affairs enforces, not the band;
4 Blood quantum rule: used by 30 bands; individuals are eligible for membership based on the number of Indian ancestors in an individual's family history. Blood quantum codes measure a person's quantum by adding the quantum of each parent and dividing by two. A typical blood quantum criterion for band membership is 50 per cent, but this is not universal in the codes. (Magnet 2003, 59)

Legally, bands could not restrict the rights of individuals who had been restored to Indian status. Canada set minimum standards for bands to follow: equality between the sexes had to be maintained, codes had to be consistent with the equality sections of the Canadian Charter of Rights and Freedoms, and a majority of electors had to consent to the decisions made about membership on or before June 27, 1987 (see Cannon 2004, 238; Indian and Northern Affairs Canada 1986, 25; Manyfingers 1986; Native Women's Association of Canada 1986, 23).

Indian bands could, however, exclude a class of people referred to as "conditional members." These individuals were predominately women who had been involuntarily enfranchised when they married non-Indian men prior to 1985 and the children of women who had been registered under section 6(2) (Gilbert 1996, 139). If a band decided to leave control over band membership with the Department of Indian Affairs or had not assumed control of membership, the department placed them on the list. However, if a band decided to take control of membership, they could be excluded by the code. Although the 1985 amendments set a minimum set of standards for membership codes, some bands exercised their legislated powers in restrictive ways, excluding women and children who had had their status restored and unleashing some of the most divisive politics yet to play out in Indian communities.

In Saskatchewan, for instance, the Sakimay Indian Band removed from its membership list a woman who had had her status restored. When she took her case to the courts, the band argued that it had the right to remove the woman from the voter's list and that that right was protected under section 35 of the Charter, the section that recognizes and affirms existing Aboriginal and treaty rights. The court responded:

> The evidence does not establish Aboriginal rights within s.35, but even if Aboriginal rights were established they would not prevail over rights assured by the Charter, for s.25 is subject to the application of s.28 in a case such as

this where the activity complained of constitutes discrimination based on gender. Section 28, it is urged, assures [sic] that provisions of the Charter, including s.25, are subject to the equal guarantee of rights to male and female persons. Moreover, s.35(4) provides that Aboriginal rights are guaranteed equally to male and female persons.[4]

The trial court concluded: "Sakimay violated its own membership code and the Indian Act under which that Code was authorized, by denying the applicant the right to vote on the basis that membership in the Band, to which she was entitled under the Band's own Code, and under the Act, was denied to her."[5] *Scrimbett v Sakimay Indian Band Council* was but one in a series of cases that would erupt after 1985, cases that pitted competing interests that had been created through the Indian Act against each other and the rights of individuals against those of the Status Indian collective (also see Dick 2006). The case symbolized the ongoing devastation left in the path of Canada's unilateral decision to claim jurisdiction for itself under section 91(24) of the Constitution Act, 1867, to define and then legislate over what it called "Indians."

The truth is that no one in the mid-1980s knew how the courts would respond if the matter of band membership came before them. They could just as likely protect the interests of the band, as was the case when a dispute over band membership erupted in my own nation. The refusal of a 50 percent majority of the electorate to participate in the band membership process had resulted in the new residency bylaw. In this case, Pamela Henderson, a non-Indigenous woman who was not a band member, disputed the new law on the grounds that she had married a Status Indian and band member. The band council had passed the residency bylaw in accordance with section 81(1) of the Indian Act, which gives band councils the authority to decide on-reserve residency so long as it is "not inconsistent with [the Act] or with any regulation made by the Governor in Council or the Minister." The Ontario Court of Justice ruled in favour of the band council. In considering the facts and evidence, it decided that it was Six Nations – not Henderson – who had the right to determine who could live on a reserve. The court concluded that a band could pass a bylaw to limit residency to band members only and for socioeconomic reasons, including the ability to deal with an influx of "non-band member spouses in terms of space and social services."[6] The court affirmed the right of Six Nations to control its own membership; however, it did so by upholding that reserve residency is not an absolute right for people with Indian status. It also contributed to a degree of uncertainty, if not insecurity, where the "acquired rights" of those of us restored to Indian status are concerned. While most of us (that is, those of us not the spouses or children of Indian men) are band members, it is unclear whether the residency bylaw could be invoked to exclude us.

It is perhaps ironic that a 50 percent majority of people at Grand River had refused to participate in the process of developing membership codes, especially in light of some of the statutes cited in the *Henderson* case, including section 91(24) of the Constitution Act, 1867, a statute premised on the incorrect assumption that we had relinquished jurisdiction over Haudenosaunee citizenship when we became "Indians." Some saw band membership codes as but another ploy by the federal government to involve us, a sovereign people, in a distinctly racialized and unbalanced conversation about our governance "as Indians." Others felt betrayed by the illusion of "power and control" being used to sell the idea of membership codes in the 1980s – an all too familiar and powerful illusion that conflates Indianness and nationhood and, for that matter, self-determination and self-government. *Self-determination, self-government, nationhood,* and *Indianness* meant different things for us as Haudenosaunee. I am not the first Haudenosaunee scholar to speak out about these issues (see Sunseri 2011; Alfred 2005; Cannon and Sunseri 2011, xv–xvi; Monture-Angus 1995; Simpson 2000). The idea being communicated by members of my band was that we had never really been Indians to begin with; therefore, we should not be engaging with Canada in colonial-inspired and disrespectful conversations about Indian policy, let alone the matter of Indian membership (Monture-Angus 1999a).

Larry Gilbert, who was once the acting registrar for the Department of Indian Affairs and Northern Development, has made a similar point regarding band control of membership, self-government, and Canada's proposal to have bands decide on the "acquired rights" of returning members. In *Entitlement to Indian Status and Membership Codes in Canada*, he perceptively writes:

> There is no doubt that Canada felt it was in a catch-22 situation [in 1985]. The people who enjoy "acquired rights" are the same people who were discriminated against under the former *Act*. The Government of Canada discriminated against them using the *Indian Act*. The only way in which Canada could appear to be conforming to human rights was to restore to those persons the same or similar rights which they were denied. The cost of making things right, however, is not born[e] by Canada, it is born[e] by the First Nations *who were equally victimized by the paternalism of Indian Affairs and by the racist laws known as the Indian Act*. Furthermore, the imposition of members with "acquired rights" *betrays the concept of control and renders the concept of self-government unmeaningful.* (Gilbert 1996, 138n15, emphasis mine)

Gilbert is not the only legal expert to comment on how Parliament fettered the ability of Indian band councils to determine Indian citizenship. Joseph Magnet, in exploring the legacy of "paternalism and racist laws," calls attention to citizenship jurisdiction – a matter he suggests is protected by legislation, notably section 35 of the Constitution Act, 1982. In commenting on *Scrimbett v Sakimay Indian Band Council* in particular, he writes:

> Bands may claim an existing Aboriginal or treaty right to determine their membership. If this claim is correct, the existing Aboriginal right would have constitutional force under s. 35(1) of the Constitution Act, 1982. A right of constitutional status should be superior to Bill C-31, which is merely statutory: the right, if established should thus trump Bill C-31's obligation to reinstate the persons who acquired rights to band membership under its terms. (Magnet 2003, 57–58)

In other words, amendments to the Indian Act did nothing to transform or dismantle the history of racialization imposed by Canada. The sections pertaining to band membership were never about self-government. The goal was to limit or undo the discrimination faced by Indians that had been involuntarily enfranchised or victimized by sexism and racialized injustice in Canada. In fact, the subject of self-government deflects attention away from the conversations we still need to be having in twenty-first-century Canada about Indianness, Indigenous sovereignty, Indigenous peoplehood, the restoration of jurisdiction, and "recognition" politics (see Andersen 2011, 2014; Coulthard 2008; Simpson 2014).

Control over band membership did not restore our jurisdiction over Indigenous citizenship or our right to be acknowledged as nations of peoples. The legislation did not revoke the category "Indian" or, for that matter, the accompanying doctrine of discovery, which is premised on Indigenous peoples' legal, economic, social, and political nonexistence as nations prior to contact (Lindberg 2010, 94). The doctrine is predicated on the erasure of Indigenous sovereignty and the declaration of lands as terra nullius (empty or unoccupied). It is settler colonialism's papal bull. Nor did control over band membership address the vocabulary of "aboriginalism" that has come to solidify itself into the constitutional law of Canada (Alfred 2005, 23; see also Alfred and Corntassel 2005). What it did do was extend to Indian Act governments the ability to more effectively administer a divide-and-conquer colonial apparatus built upon the concept of Indianness – most notably, the ability to legislate some of us outside of the Indian collective because of our (grand) mothers' gender and intermarriage.

Glen Coulthard, a Dené scholar, provides the insights necessary to understand why some bands became so invested in the development of Indian codes in the 1980s and 1990s. Citing the work of Frantz Fanon (1967), he writes in "Beyond Recognition" (2008, 191):

> Fanon first persuasively argued that the long-term stability of a colonial structure of dominance relies as much on the "internalization" of the racist forms of asymmetrical and non-mutual modes of recognition, either imposed or bestowed on the Indigenous population, as it does on brute force ... In contexts of domination such as colonialism, not only are the terms of recognition usually determined by, and in the interests of, the colonizer, but also over time colonized populations tend to develop what he called "psycho-affective" attachments to these master-sanctioned forms of recognition, and that this subjective attachment is essential in maintaining the economic and political structure of colonizer/colonized relations themselves.

Following Fanon and Coulthard, I suggest that band membership is a mechanism of control and power wielded strategically by Canada to regulate identity. It draws not from the brute force that is settler colonialism but from the internalized mindset that is Indianness. Discussions about band membership draw our attention away from the fact that it should be nationhood, not Indianness, that defines our relationship with one another and with Canada.

The 1985 amendments created a seemingly untenable situation for Status Indians. Women and their children who had their status restored were refused services – including postsecondary educational assistance, on-reserve housing, health services, and welfare – until membership codes were passed (see Holmes 1987, 20, 35; see also Furi and Wherrett 2003, 10). In some communities, new (and restored) Indians were resented for the financial burden that they presented to Indian bands (Green 1997; Indian and Northern Affairs 1990). Frequently, the anger and hostility arising from years of sex discrimination and our racialization as Indians was displaced onto one another as Indians (Cannon 1993; Small 1993). Bands were placed into a position of having to accommodate those who had been involuntarily enfranchised, despite an ongoing and state-inspired shortage of lands and resources. And they were told that amendments to the Indian Act would "correct for historical injustices" stemming from sexism, as if sexism shared no relationship with racialization (see Indian and Northern Affairs Canada 1990). As political scientist Joyce Green (1985, 93) has noted, bands were placed in charge of expiating the past patriarchal sins of Parliament.

THE 1985 AMENDMENTS to the Indian Act sparked a number of court battles over the rights of Indian bands and Indians that were rooted in the legislation's residual discrimination and symbolized the devastation and divisive politics that followed from Canada's ongoing and unilateral attempts to define and legislate over what it called "Indians." The cases sought to determine the rights of non-band members, the rights of reinstated persons, the voting rights of off-reserve members, and the right of band councils to determine membership.

Goodswimmer v Canada (1994) involved Darlene Desjarlais, a non-Indian, non-band member of the Sturgeon Lake Indian Band in Alberta, who had been elected to band council chief, sparking controversy in the community. Appeals were filed with the minister of the Department of Indian Affairs. The minister's office responded by stating that Desjarlais, in having married a Status Indian male and in having resided with him on the reserve, ought to have been able to become (and remain) the chief of her husband's Indian band. At stake in *Goodswimmer* was the right of a non-Indian and non-band member to participate in band council governance as chief, and by extension, to participate in the band's internal affairs. In the eyes of the minister, there was nothing that made this unlawful. The rules established through legislation prevented non-band members from becoming band councillors, but no such restriction existed for the position of band council chief.

The trial court in *Goodswimmer* upheld the minister's position, concluding that the rules of eligibility and nomination outlined in section 75 of the Indian Act pertained only to band councillors. The court determined that, legislatively, a candidate for chief did not need to be an elector.[7] And the conclusion reached by the court was final. The case was dismissed by the Federal Court of Appeal on March 21, 1995, and by the Supreme Court in 1997 (Furi and Wherrett 2003, 16). *Goodswimmer* stood as a reminder to us as Indians that the terms by which we are able to govern ourselves are set out in the Indian Act and that, quite often, final authority rests with the minister of Indian Affairs or the courts. Canada has sought to limit the power of Indian band councils, either by making it possible to outlaw or depose those not following the Indian Act elected system or through rulings issued by courts. Darlene Desjarlais's appointment also stands as evidence that Indian bands are by no means insular or untouched entities. Settler women live in Status Indian communities, and they have children and relatives who are Status Indians. They influence decision making, and they sometimes administer Status Indian communities as Indian chiefs. Their very existence serves as evidence that it is neither cultural heritage nor affiliation that determines identity and belonging but rather where women stand in relation to Indian and non-Indian men (see Dick 2006, 112–13).

The rights of reinstated band members came before the courts when the Canadian Human Rights Tribunal heard the matter of *Courtois v Canada, Minister of Indian Affairs and Northern Development* (1991).[8] The case centred on the right of reinstated members to secure educational assistance. The claimants were refused services normally provided to band members, namely, entry and admission to band-operated schools. The band had implemented a two-year moratorium on providing assistance to reinstated members, and it argued that it was well within its rights to do so. The plaintiffs argued the opposite, claiming that the moratorium constituted discrimination on the grounds of sexism and marital status. The tribunal agreed with the claimants, concluding that they were entitled to band-funded services on the reserve. Furthermore, it concluded that bands were obligated to provide these services because the funding is sourced, not by them but by the federal government (that is, the Department of Indian and Northern Affairs). This fact, according to the tribunal, in turn obligated the band to provide funds to all Indians residing at the reserve, regardless of band membership. Foreshadowing the now infamous words used by Justice Muldoon in the later case *Sawridge Band v Canada*, the court took the position that "whoever pays the piper calls the tune."[9] However, as ha dih nyoh scholar Thomas Isaac (1995, 1) commented, this approach is blind to historical considerations, especially the issuing of "benefits, monetary or otherwise" that have come to impact and influence interpersonal relationships, Indigenous sovereignty, and decision making.

The reality is that we are not in a position to dispute the outcome of the *Courtois* decision so long as we are Indians and so long as the funding for band members is established and administered by Indigenous and Northern Affairs Canada. And there is no mechanism to disrupt the historical amnesia and politics that work to fuel animosity between us as Indians. *Courtois* is evidence of the erosion of harmonious social and gender relations that accompanied colonialism and racialization, the loss of economic control, and the imposition of patriarchy. In this context, the involuntarily enfranchised – reinstated women and their children – are sometimes seen as outsiders. What served initially to separate us from the "status collective" was (and is) rarely acknowledged. Patriarchal prerogatives combine with limited economic resources to make the effects of discrimination especially intense and damaging.

The controversy surrounding the matter of reinstated members pales in comparison with the reaction that followed rulings that made it possible for off-reserve Indians to vote in band elections. Until 1999, the right to vote in band elections was restricted by the Indian Act to on-reserve residents. In *Corbiere v Canada (Minister of Indian and Northern Affairs)* (1999), the Supreme Court of Canada was asked to make a ruling on the rights of non-resident band members to participate in band governance and elections. The court was asked if either the trial or appeal courts had erred in deciding that section 77(1) of the 1985 Indian Act – the section requiring that only band members who are "ordinarily resident on the reserve" be allowed to participate in band council elections – constituted discrimination towards off-reserve residents under section 15 of the Charter. The court upheld the lower court judgments that it did constitute discrimination and went further, adding that "aboriginality-residence" can work as a form of discrimination analogous to that of the enumerated grounds listed under section 15 (that is, race, national or ethnic origin, colour, religion, sex, and so on). In the words of the court: "To say that a ground of distinction is an analogous ground is merely to identify a type of decision-making that is suspect because it often leads to discrimination and denial of substantive equality."[10] *Corbiere* not only changed the political landscape in the 1990s, it added an additional grounds for discrimination (residency) under the Charter of Rights and Freedoms. It worked to extend the rights of off-reserve band members, which would become "a very litigious issue" in the twenty-first century (Isaac 1994, 55).

The *Corbiere* decision might well be regarded as a progressive one. The judgment illuminated a history of discriminatory laws that had worked to legislate some Indigenous people outside of the Indian collective. More importantly, it worked to dispel the myth that living off the reserve was always voluntary. In fact, the court detailed the circumstances (legislative, economic, and resources-based) that had forced *all our relations* to leave reserves in Canada and noted that lack of residency in no way signalled a lack of interest or connection to the reserve community. To exclude off-reserve members was therefore tantamount to "forcing band members to choose between living on the reserve and exercising their political rights or living off reserve and renouncing the exercise of their political rights."[11]

The court drew from the *Report of the Royal Commission on Aboriginal Peoples* (Canada 1996) in reaching its decision. The commission had shown that off-reserve residents do not simply assimilate into mainstream society. Many of us maintain active and meaningful connections to our reserves and ought, therefore, to be able to participate meaningfully in them. *Corbiere* affirmed the right of off-reserve Indians – many of them women and involuntarily enfranchised people – to belong in Indian communities. Because many Status Indians participate and, indeed, invest in our ancestral homelands economically, *Corbiere* affirmed the right of off-reserve people to a sense of "cultural identity" afforded by the reserve's familial, ritual, and ceremonial underpinnings. The case spoke to matters of identity and belonging and limited the power of band councils to discriminate against off-reserve members. *Sawridge Band v Canada* (1996), which considered the rights of reinstated women and the rights of band councils, likewise limited the ability of band councils to determine membership. The case involved three bands in Alberta – Sawridge, Ermineskin, and Sarcee – that challenged sections 8 and 14.3 of the Indian Act on the grounds that they infringed upon the right of bands to determine their own membership.[12] The sections require Indian governments to maintain a band list and to allow individuals to make grievances against band membership codes on the grounds of discrimination. In general, these sections were said by the bands to be in violation of the "existing aboriginal and treaty rights" guaranteed by section 35 of the Constitution Act, 1982, which reads:

(1) The existing aboriginal and treaty rights of the aboriginal peoples of Canada are hereby recognized and affirmed.

(2) In this Act, "Aboriginal Peoples of Canada" includes the Indian, Inuit and Métis peoples of Canada.

(3) For greater certainty, in subsection (1) "treaty rights" includes rights that now exist by way of land claims agreements or may be so acquired.

(4) Notwithstanding any other provision of this Act, the aboriginal and treaty rights referred to in subsection (1) are guaranteed equally to male and female persons.

The Sawridge, Ermineskin, and Sarcee Bands argued that the ability to decide band membership is a matter of governance

extending from time immemorial and that it is a constitution-
ally protected Aboriginal right. The right, they argued, entitled
all three bands to carry on their marital custom of "woman
follows man," a tradition written into their membership codes
that conflicted with the rights restored to Indian women and
children under the 1985 amendments. The Indian Act, they
argued, infringed on the bands' Aboriginal rights, as did the
rights of individuals – in this case, those belonging to reinstated women and children.

The bands also applied for a declaration stating that the
addition of "new" reinstated members to the Sawridge,
Ermineskin, and Sarcee Bands constituted an imposition
and interference with their rights to freedom of association
under section 2(d) of the Constitution Act, 1982, which reads:

> Everyone has the following fundamental freedoms:
> (a) freedom of conscience and religion;
> (b) freedom of thought, belief, opinion and expression,
>   including freedom of the press and other media of
>   communication;
> (c) freedom of peaceful assembly; and
> (d) freedom of association.

The trial court found that neither of these objections was
defensible and dismissed all claims with costs. It concluded
that there were no existing treaty or Aboriginal rights to
determine membership in Indian communities. Had such
rights ever existed, they had been extinguished by federal
statute – in particular section 91(24) of the Constitution
Act, 1867. The bands' right to determine their own membership had, furthermore, been extinguished by Treaties 6,
7, and 8. In what stands today as one of the more controver-
sial dimensions of the *Sawridge* case, Justice Muldoon
reasoned:

It was quite obvious and well understood by the Indian parties to all three treaties that the Government of Canada was thereafter to control their band and reserve membership, because the government was committed to pay Indians forever as an eternal charge on taxpayers. Clearly the government was committed also to control who was to be paid individually, and who was not entitled to be paid individually. The Indians were neither simpletons nor crazy. They well understood that "money talks" and that "whoever pays the piper, calls the tune."[13]

This is but one of several excerpts from *Sawridge* that drew the shock and attention of Indigenous peoples and legal scholars in the 1990s. In what amounted to a very selective reading of the treaty-making process, the court ruled that there was no Aboriginal right to determine band membership, least of all one that had been established by a statute or treaty (Isaac 1995; Ratushny 2000).[14]

The *Sawridge* judgment also condemned the inequitable treatment of women under the bands' membership codes. Justice Muldoon struck down the bands' marital custom of "woman follows man," arguing that section 35(4) of the Constitution Act extinguished this custom. Muldoon added that regardless of how the marital custom of "woman follows man" might have operated in the past, "it can be clearly seen that the marital custom, the so-called Aboriginal and treaty rights which permit an Indian husband to bring his non-Indian wife into residence on a reserve, but which forbid an Indian wife from so bringing her non-Indian husband are extinguished utterly by s-s. 35(4)."[15] Justice Muldoon also condemned the idea of blood quantum. He reasoned that the bands had used the concept to determine identity and band membership and, using provocative language, concluded that blood quantum effects the worst sorts of racism:

"'Blood quantum' is a highly fascist and racist notion, and puts its practitioners on the path of the Nazi Party led by the late, most unlamented Adolf Hitler."[16] This statement and others led the bands to appeal the decision. On June 3, 1997, the Federal Court of Appeal agreed that Justice Muldoon's comments on racism and Aboriginal rights as a "special status" in particular afforded a "reasonable apprehension of bias" on the part of the Trial Court (see Magnet 2003, 58; Ratushny 2000).[17] The Court of Appeal ordered a retrial, but the Supreme Court of Canada refused leave to appeal in December 1997. *Sawridge Band v Canada* has not been heard again, at least in its original form.

The *Sawridge* decision was a significant piece of case law, especially in terms of addressing the matter of racism. However, racism was not raised as an issue that Canada itself should address, particularly the Indian Act's role in making it possible for Indigenous peoples to think of themselves and others in racialized terms. In fact, the court upheld the right of Parliament under section 91(24) of the Constitution Act, 1867, to define and then legislate over us as "Indians." The court also condemned the patriarchy that has taught some men to disrespect our (grand)mothers and to see them as outsiders, but it did nothing to draw attention to its colonial and racialized origins or to correct the loss of land that had so efficiently helped to consolidate patriarchy in many communities.

Sawridge showed just how far patriarchy has come to (re)shape, change, or destroy the gender balance in Indigenous communities. Women were said to be threatening the status collective – not because men were opposed to gender equality, or had anything against women personally, but because they wanted to protect the cultural integrity of Indian bands. At various points, they referred to the practice of "woman follows man" as a "marital custom," as if the years of sexism brought on by colonialism had not changed the meaning and impact of marriage. The custom of "woman follows man" was said to constitute an authentic or traditional practice immune from human rights–based challenges or criticism because it was so vital to their culture. However, it was, instead, a highly suspect version of tradition invoked to protect discriminatory practices aimed at women and their children (see Cannon 1995, 103; see also Green 1997). The judgment thus worked to disempower women by disregarding how patriarchy – historically and in modern times – has transformed women's status in communities. It prevented Indigenous people from seeing how sexism impacts us all.

Sawridge Band v Canada in fact revealed that sex discrimination has to do with a lot more than women or gender. Sexism affects the entire status collective, including men, because we, too, are treated unequally – not only because we are Indians but also, in many cases, because our (grand)fathers are white and our (grand)mothers are Indian (also see Dick 2006, 112). It is therefore illogical to interpret *Sawridge* as a case launched to protect Indian reserves from outside cultural influence. If that were true, our aunties, friends, and other relatives – many of them settler women whom we visit and who reside on reserves with our male relatives – would have been thrown out or seen as threatening the cultural integrity of bands in Canada long before the issue hit the courts in the 1990s in cases such as *Henderson*.

THE CASE LAW PERTAINING to Indians and Indian status following the 1985 amendments to the Indian Act represented a turning point in the history of racialization, sexism, and citizenship injustice in Canada. People now sought resolutions to colonial grievances through the Canadian Charter of Rights and Freedoms. At the same time, some people grew increasingly skeptical of the Charter, questioning whether it ought to be used to resolve grievances that had stemmed from colonialism. Some legal scholars wrote of the contradiction that arises when an Indigenous person, feeling dissatisfied with an Indian Act band council government or decision, turns to the Charter for recognition of his or her individual rights (see Mercredi and Turpel 1993; Nahanee 1993; Turpel 1993). Their concerns fed into and emerged out of debates that raged during the constitutional negotiations of the early 1990s.

In 1992, the federal and provincial governments put forward the Charlottetown Accord, a package of proposed amendments to the Constitution. The accord would have substantially altered the status of Indians in Canada by making any form of self-government – including the inherent right to self-government – subject to the Charter's provisions (Isaac 1993, 628). In principle, this meant the Charter would have continued to provide a viable route for the settling of human rights grievances among Indigenous peoples and women. Although the accord was rejected in a national referendum on October 26, 1992, it raised a number of concerns in Status Indian communities about the rights of individuals overriding those of the collective. The Assembly of First Nations (AFN) saw the proposed amendments in the Charlottetown Accord as detrimental to tradition and cultural autonomy. The Native Women's Association of Canada (NWAC) took the opposite position, noting that if self-government remained subject to the Charter, it would help to ensure the social and political rights of women. They argued that there could be no viable collective without safeguarding the rights of individuals, that seeking to protect the latter would only work to bolster the former.

The NWAC was clear in stating its position on the application and use of the Charter. In speaking on behalf of its constituents, it felt that any form of self-government needed to protect the equality rights of women under sections 15 and 35(4) of the Charter – rights that had been routinely denied historically. As an organization that represented Indian women subject to federal legislation, the NWAC perceived the Charter's jurisdiction as weighing heavily towards ensuring equality rights. In their testimony to the Supreme Court of Canada in 1992, they explained:

> Without the *Charter,* Aboriginal women will be helpless to resist the discriminatory actions of Band Councils, or any other form of self-government to be developed. This is because the Canadian Human Rights Act does not apply to the Indian Act, and provincial human rights codes are also inapplicable for jurisdictional reasons ... If those who advocate that the *Charter* not apply to Aboriginal self-government are successful, it will mean that Aboriginal women have no protection under any instrument guaranteeing our basic human and equality rights.[18]

The NWAC's position gained strength from a growing realization that the history of sex discrimination, as it had been created and institutionalized through the Indian Act and band councils, required attention and scrutiny. If self-government was not subject to the Charter, the organization argued, this would amount to a blessing and reaffirmation of patriarchy in Status Indian communities (see Nahanee 1993, 372; Native Women's Association of Canada 1992a, 14; Weaver 1993, 129). As the NWAC (1992b, 11) wrote: "Stripped of equality by patriarchal laws which created 'Male privilege' as the norm on reserve lands, Aboriginal women have a tremendous struggle to regain their social position. We want the *Canadian Charter of Rights and Freedoms* to apply to Aboriginal governments." Just as in the 1970s, Indigenous women's political aspirations in the 1990s had two goals: to protect their legal and political rights as historically enfranchised peoples and to combat Western patriarchy. Given their history of having suffered patriarchal subjugation at the hands of both the federal and band-level governments, their position on having the Charter apply to Indians cannot be dismissed as untenable.

The AFN, however, held firm in its opposition. Notwithstanding the concerns of the NWAC, the AFN saw the Charter as but one more assault on Indigenous cultural autonomy. Far from simply being a reflection of male bias, the organization argued, their concern was with the preservation of tradition and culture. The AFN acquired support for its position from legal and academic experts such as Mary Ellen Turpel (see Turpel 1989–90, 1991). As Ovide Mercredi, national chief of the AFN, and Turpel (1993, 98) wrote:

> To help people understand the basis of our resistance to the current *Charter* ... let me make it clear that it has nothing to do with wanting to undermine or diminish women. We are not opposed to gender equality. We are not opposed to the individual freedom or choice of any First Nations citizen. We want to guard against the destruction of traditional forms of governing ourselves and resolving disputes.

The Charter, they argued, as an undeniably foreign and Eurocentric piece of legislation, represented a threat to the culture of Indigenous peoples (Isaac 1993; Turpel 1989–90).

In many respects, the Charter is incongruent with Indigenous principles and beliefs – for instance, its introductory preamble refers to Canada's being "founded upon principles that recognize the supremacy of God and the rule of law." While the notion of Canada being "founded" negates recognition of Indigenous peoples as first peoples, the reference to the "supremacy of God" denies Indigenous spirituality. The reference to the rule of law, furthermore, suggests that the law is impartial when in fact Eurocentrism has had a substantial bearing on judicial decisions in Canada. Judges are by no means impartial, detached, or able to reason through abstractions provided by the law alone. The outcome of *Lavell* in the 1970s is a case in point.

The phrase "supremacy of God and the rule of law" implies that equality under the law is possible. But it fails to acknowledge that not all individuals are equal to begin with. Is it possible to make Indigenous peoples, who are all too often unequal in life, equal under the law? In guaranteeing equal protection and equal benefit of the law without discrimination based on race, sex, age, ethnic origin, colour, and so on, section 15 of the Charter suggests that it is. But, as ha dih nyoh legal scholar Michael Mandel (1989, 240) notes: "It is no accident that the *Charter's* list of the items according to which we must be equal in law are the very things according to which we are unequal in life." By what criteria or standards should a court measure "equality"? Does the Charter seek to make Indigenous peoples equal to one another? Does it seek to make Indigenous people equal to non-Indigenous people? Or does it propose both? Having access to equal treatment and social justice in life is one thing; whether they can be attained through a legal approach, as is implicitly proposed in the Charter, is another.

A liberal approach to equality rests upon the idea of sameness – a measure that suppresses difference by making settler society the norm against which "difference" or "equality" is measured. As Anishinaabe scholar John Borrows (1994, 28) wrote at the height of the controversy over the Charter, "The only standard the court can recognize in the absence of contrary evidence [is] that of Canadian society at large." When Turpel (1993, 185) wrote of these matters of equality, difference, and sameness, she asked:

What are the implications of the mentality which suggests that the goal for society is equality with (White) men? To me, to be a First Nations person in Canada means to be free to exist politically and culturally (these are not separate concepts): to be free to understand our roles according to our own cultural and political systems and not according to a value system imposed upon us by the Indian Act for over 100 years, nor by role definition accepted in the Anglo-European culture. This means that men are not, and therefore cannot be, the measure of all things.

By proposing equality the way it does, the Charter was not seen in the 1990s by Indigenous scholars and the AFN as recognizing the distinct nature – their unique differences, positions, and characteristics – of Indigenous peoples.

Some Status Indians suggested that there was something fundamentally wrong with Indigenous peoples' appropriating the rights discourse of the Charter. In fact, some argued that it makes little sense to resolve human rights grievances through the Charter, especially since many of them (grievances relating to Indian status, band membership, and sexism) were created by Canada in the first place. The AFN took this position, questioning whether the Charter could be used to secure the rights of women. Mercredi and Turpel (1993, 97) wrote: "The government wants to apply the *Charter* to solve the human rights problems it created when it imposed the Indian Act. Many First Nations people question why we should allow government to impose more unilateral legislation as a way of solving the problems they generated in the first place." They continued:

The *Charter* should not be seen as a panacea for the ills of society. If the government plans to impose its solution on us, we will resist ... It is in this context that we have argued against the *Charter*, not because we are opposed to gender equality, even though some would present it this way. Where did our gender inequality come from? From the Indian Act, and not from our traditions. (Mercredi and Turpel 1993, 103)

People stood in opposition to the Charter in the 1990s because it represented a further legal encroachment upon our sovereignty as Indigenous peoples. To accept the application and utility of the Charter is to seek and affirm judicial solutions when, historically, the inequality we face as peoples – including gender inequality – can be traced back to settler colonialism and has since been administered through Parliament and legislation. To that end, it is Parliament, not the courts, that ought to take the lead in resolving human rights disputes and issues.

The Charter was also opposed in the 1990s because it prioritizes the rights of the individual and, in the eyes of some Status Indians, the individual rights of Indigenous women should not take priority over the rights of Indigenous peoples as a collective. This sentiment was captured in a presentation made to the Standing Committee on Indian Women and the Indian Act. Representatives of the AFN explained:

As Indian people, we cannot afford to have individual rights override collective rights. Our societies have never been structured that way, unlike yours, and that is where the clash comes as well with the *Charter of Rights* issue under the constitution. If you isolate the individual rights from the collective rights, then you are heading down another path that is even more discriminatory.[19]

In other words, the Charter was opposed because of its liberal, individual rights–based orientation. Legal and academic theorists in particular argued that placing the rights of individuals before the rights of the status collective would ultimately undermine the rights of Indigenous peoples as a group. They argued that any form of self-government would be compromised if subjected to a culturally dominant human-rights paradigm such as the Charter and that any use of the Charter would subject Indigenous peoples to the status quo (see Boldt and Long 1985, 177). In fact, it would call into question the "humanitarian integrity" of Indigenous peoples under self-government (Isaac 1993, 628). Over time, legal theorists held that the use of Charter rights discourse, especially in the settling of intergroup and human rights disputes, would weaken the autonomous development of Indigenous peoples. Turpel (1989–90, 40) wrote: "It is difficult for a culturally distinct people to define the trajectory of its own development if individuals from within ... the culture can challenge collective decisions on the basis that they infringe their individual rights under the *Charter* in the Canadian legal system which does not understand, or give priority to collective goals."

Human rights discourse was thus seen as a detriment to the collective rights of Indigenous peoples in the 1990s. Legal theorists had become all too familiar with the case law pertaining to sexism, the Indian Act, and band membership codes. Many worried where the case law would lead when it came to intragroup grievances, which had become commonplace (see Dick 2006; Green 1997). In the eyes of some theorists, these were disputes best settled by the community itself, not the courts (see Hammersmith 1992, 56–57; Turpel 1989–90, 42). Turpel (1989–90, 41) argued that seeking judicial resolution to disputes "would be a dangerous opening for a ruling by a Canadian court on individual versus collective rights within an Aboriginal community [and] would also break down community methods of dispute-resolution and restoration, or place limits on the re-establishment of such methods." The AFN insisted that the rights of women flowed from Aboriginal rights, not the Charter, and that individual rights should not override the rights of the collective. It would have been a persuasive argument were it not for the fact that bands such as Sawridge sought to defend their custom, tradition, and rights as Aboriginal peoples under the Charter.

THE 1990S PLAYED HOST to a number of contradictions where the Charter was concerned. Paramount among them was the way it was opposed in the name of preserving traditional methods of governance and dispute resolution.[20] There was an inherent irony within these all-or-nothing politics in that they precluded discussion of how Indigenous organizations are – and have been – modelled on a foreign and imposed method of political organization. As Patricia Monture-Angus (1999b, 148) writes, Indian governments "cannot fully give voice to tradition," nor are they "necessarily about fully reaching out to the goals of emancipation, freedom and independence." The irony was that Status Indian organizations were making appeals to tradition even though they themselves were symbols of imposed Indian Act governance. In the discussions that ensued, we were prevented as "Status Indians" from having our sovereignty, which we share with Canada, legally acknowledged and affirmed (see Fleras 2009, 78). There were no discussions about what it was that had preceded Indian Act governance or, more importantly, about the colonial policy that sought to outlaw it. Status organizations did little to acknowledge or challenge the impact that colonialism had had upon them, nor did they recognize their own embodiment as creatures of statutes, as remnants of colonial-based and imposed systems of government. Thus, Indian governments themselves appropriated human rights discourse.

"Tradition" in the 1990s was paraded in suspect ways. It was not clear whether people were speaking of the diverse and varied practices that had existed prior to settler colonialism or of those that had been brought on by the Indian Act or with colonial influence. Following European contact, some traditions were nothing more than what Eric Hobsbawm and Terence Ranger (1983, 1–14) refer to as invented traditions. A problem arose in the 1990s when invented traditions such as "woman follows man" were used to obscure the maintenance of heteropatriarchy. It was as if our traditions were static and unchanging – untouched by the history of sexism contained in, and later internalized because of, Canada's Indian policy. Appeals to tradition exonerated Status Indian governments from taking responsibility for modern-day sexism. As Ovide Mercredi declared, "gender inequality comes from the Indian Act and not from our traditions" (Mercredi and Turpel 1993, 103). Such invocations were useful politically, but they did nothing to address the degree to which patriarchy had (re)structured our communities (Cannon 1995, 104; Green 1997, 146). As Borrows (1994, 31) wrote of the contradiction, "it is no longer enough to say that the *Indian Act* was responsible." Appeals to tradition not only obfuscated the way that sexism affected the lives of Indian men and women differently, they also deflected attention away from what happened – and needed to happen – in our communities in terms of responsibility and action. Racialization and sexism needed to be recognized as the means through which our dispossession had ensued.

The failure to acknowledge the relationship between racialization and sexism was evident in 1990s case law. Although the courts may have worked diligently and in progressive ways to prevent, denounce, or reverse the patriarchy that had overtaken some communities as a result of the Indian Act, they generally refused to address the matter of racialized injustice (i.e., Indianness) as well as lands appropriation and dispossession, which were realized through sexism. The law is by no means a transformative arbiter of justice (P. Monture 2006). The goal in these cases was to lessen the effects of sexism and other forms of discrimination; however, they created new (or recast) forms of discrimination, including the refusal to address the category "Indian." The courts also failed to take up the issues of jurisdiction, Indigenous sovereignty, and citizenship. Although they condemned band councils for the racism inherent in the concept of blood quantum and other band membership codes, there was no discussion of how to legally restore jurisdiction over matters of citizenship to Indigenous nations. Nor did courts in cases such as *Sawridge* work to renounce the power that Canada had granted to itself under section 91(24) of the Constitution Act, 1867, to define and then legislate over what it called Indians.

The extent to which this power is entrenched was recently driven home when an Indigenous woman successfully challenged the Indian Act's "unstated paternity" policy in the courts. She won her case, but the case failed to convince Canada to amend or retract the Indian Act. In 2001, Lynn Gehl, a citizen of the Algonquin Nation, took the matter of unknown or unstated paternity before the Ontario courts, arguing that the policy was discriminatory because it penalized those with unknown fathers in their family trees. She argued that the inequality brought on by a "negative presumption of paternity" by the Registrar had caused her father to be deemed ineligible for Indian registration. The Registrar had refused him Indian status because his father's identity was missing on his birth certificate. The Registrar therefore assumed that Gehl's paternal grandfather had been a non-Indian.[21] Gehl argued, however, that her paternal grandmother was an Indian entitled to registration under section 6(1). Therefore, her father, as a child who had one parent entitled to be registered under section 6(1), should have been registered under section 6(2).

Although her case should have caused the courts to revisit the law, the Ontario Trial Court found that there was no discrimination and that the Registrar had merely been acting in accordance with the Indian Act. Justice Swinton held that the denial of status had resulted not from individual discretion or an unconstitutional decision on behalf of the Registrar but from the Indian Act itself – from a statutory framework that required government bureaucrats to determine whether a child had one or two parents who are (or were) entitled to registration under section 6(1). The court concluded that the proper avenue for legal redress would be through litigation challenging the constitutionality of the Indian Act under the Charter of Rights and Freedoms, section 52(1) of which reads: "The Constitution of Canada is the supreme law of Canada, and any law that is inconsistent with the provisions of the Constitution is, to the extent of the inconsistency, of no force or effect." As *Gehl v Canada* made clear, the 1985 amendments had not corrected for our involuntary enfranchisement as Indians.

Along with Gehl, the Assembly of First Nations and the Native Women's Association of Canada initiated awareness campaigns to draw attention to how unknown and unstated paternity affects status claims (on Gehl's activism, see Perkel 2017). Gehl finally won her case in the Ontario Court of Appeal on April 20, 2017.[22] Justice Sharpe reasoned that while Gehl had framed her action as a constitutional challenge, she was really contesting the reasonableness of the Registrar's policy. He then proceeded to review its reasonableness and concluded that proof of identity is harder to establish for fathers and that women may have valid reasons to not disclose the identity of their child's father. The policy disadvantaged Indigenous women and "failed to take into account the equality-enhancing values and remedial objectives underlying the 1985 amendments and was therefore unreasonable."[23] Gehl had been without justice since the 1985 Indian Act amendments. Despite the ruling, Canada has not amended or retracted the Indian Act, leaving us with the impression, as Indians, that all further grievances concerning the matter will need to be litigated on a very expensive case-by-case basis (see also Galloway 2017a, 2017b).

Sexism, Indigenous Sovereignty, and *McIvor v The Registrar,* 2007–09

THAT THE LAW IN Canada is not a transformative arbiter of justice but rather actively invested in the colonial project and the affirmation of settler sovereignty became quite evident when Sharon McIvor's case, which centred on whether section 6 of the Indian Act discriminated against women, finally came before the courts in the early 2000s. Although the case had the potential to correct the history of sex discrimination in the Indian Act and reconcile the racialized injustice realized through sexism, it ultimately failed. As Patricia Monture (2006, 90) argues in "Standing against Canadian Law," the law is of only limited use to Indigenous people when it comes to matters of Indian status, citizenship, and sovereignty or the resolution of colonial grievances:

> The reason why Canadian law does not fully work for resolving Aboriginal claims – including those fundamentally concerning Aboriginal women – is quite simple. Canadian courts owe their origin to British notions of when a nation is sovereign. It is from Canadian sovereignty that Canadian courts owe their existence. Courts, therefore, cannot question the very source of their existence without fully jeopardizing their own being. Courts cannot be forced to look

at issues about legitimacy (or, more appropriately, the lack thereof) of Canadian sovereignty as against the claims of Aboriginal sovereignties. The result is that Aboriginal claimants (women, men, and nations) can never hope to litigate the issue that is at the very heart of our claims.

One should always, therefore, look upon the law with a formidable degree of skepticism, especially where the matter of Indian status is concerned.

As I'll show, *McIvor v The Registrar* (2007) resulted in a condemnation of the legislative treatment of Status Indians since 1985 and the introduction of Bill C-3 and the passage of the Gender Equity in Indian Registration Act.[1] However, the legacy of inequality surrounding Indian status and federal recognition was not remedied by the *McIvor* case. Nor have amendments to existing legislation reconciled the matter of Indian status injustices (Canada 2010; Indigenous Bar Association 2010).[2] The Gender Equity in Indian Registration Act grants section 6(1) status to the children of out-marrying women, section 6(2) status to their grandchildren, and no status to their great-grandchildren. The act did not eradicate the two-generation cut off – it merely suspended it for one generation. It is now the great-grandchildren of out-marrying women (but not of men) who face legal assimilation (Canadian Bar Association 2010).[3] Thus, the courts failed, not by refusing to hear arguments about the sex discrimination contained within the Indian Act but by concluding that sex discrimination is the only injustice facing our (grand)mothers, even though they are "Indians."

ON JUNE 8, 2007, Justice Carol Ross of the Supreme Court of British Columbia issued the landmark *McIvor* decision. It was the very first case to challenge sex discrimination in the 1985 amendments to the Indian Act. The plaintiffs, Sharon McIvor and her son, Charles Jacob Grismer (referred to as Jacob), submitted that the amendments were, from the very start, incomplete and remedial legislation. They maintained that the 1985 Indian Act violated their guarantee of equality under section 15 of the Charter on two grounds: (1) it discriminated on the basis of sex, given that the ability to confer Indian status depended on whether one had descended from the maternal or paternal line, and (2) it discriminated on the basis of sex, given that male and female Indians who married non-Indians were treated differently.

The trial court favoured both arguments and agreed with the plaintiffs that, historically, the Indian Act had privileged the male line of descent. Justice Ross stated:

> I have concluded that s. 6 of the 1985 Act violates s. 15(1) of the Charter in that it discriminates between matrilineal and patrilineal descendants born prior to April 17, 1985, in the conferring of Indian status, and discriminates between descendants born prior to April 17, 1985, of Indian women who married non-Indian men, and the descendants of Indian men who married non-Indian women. I have concluded that these provisions are not saved by s. 1.[4]

Section 6(2) was found to be particularly repugnant because it gave fewer rights and denied status to the descendants of female Indians. In reaching this conclusion, Ross suggested that steps must be taken judicially to reconcile these matters of discrimination. In what might well be regarded as one of the most striking dimensions of the case, she issued an expansive remedy: "S. 6 of the 1985 Act is of no force and effect insofar, and only insofar, as it authorizes the differential treatment of Indian men and Indian women born prior to April 17, 1985, and matrilineal and patrilineal descendants born prior to April 17, 1985, in the conferring of Indian status."[5]

In rendering section 6 of the Indian Act of no force or effect, the *McIvor* decision meant three things. First, women who had lost Indian status upon marriage to non-Indian or unregistered men could reacquire it under the same section as men who had married non-Indian or unregistered spouses before April 1985. Second, descendants of women and men could be registered under the same section of the act. Third, and finally, it allowed the grandchildren of out-marrying women to register for Indian status (National Centre for First Nations Governance 2009, 4). The *McIvor* decision stood to increase the Status Indian population, a prospect that has never been part of the vision of the settler state. Not surprisingly, just one week after it was delivered, the minister of Indian affairs, Jim Prentice, was quoted in the *Globe and Mail* as saying that his government would appeal it (Curry 2007).

The BC Court of Appeal answered this call of government and delivered its decision on April 6, 2009, less than two years after the case had originally gone to trial. On appeal, Justices Groberman, Newbury, and Tysoe upheld the finding of the trial court that the Indian Act violated section 15 of the Charter. The court, however, issued its judgment on much narrower grounds. First, the appeal court asked whether the inequality between matrilineal and patrilineal descendants represented an enumerated grounds for discrimination based on sex or an analogous grounds based on lineage.[6] Second, the court reduced the scope of the remedy offered by Justice Ross by narrowly defining, and then comparing, the wrongful discrimination experienced by the descendants of out-marrying women to a small subset of individuals who had descended from men.

At the trial, Justice Ross accepted that Grismer would have been a Status Indian had he not been the descendant of a woman. The trial court decided to compare the experience of Grismer and all descendants who had lost status because of their mother's decision to marry out with that of all individuals who had descended from men prior to April 17, 1985. On appeal, however, the court opted to restrict the comparator group in question, focusing only on individuals impacted by the "double mother" rule – that is, persons who were reinstated after the 1985 amendments under section 6(1)(c). The double mother rule had been introduced in 1951 under amendments to the Indian Act. As ha dih nyoh lawyer and activist Mary Eberts (2010, 19) notes, the rule was "the first and only pre-1985 imposition on what had previously been the male progenitor's untrammeled ability to confer Indian status on children born inside marriage." The double mother rule provided that "if a child's mother and paternal grandmother did not have a right to Indian status, other than by virtue of having married an Indian man, the child only had Indian status up to the age of 21."[7] The argument went that the rule restricted the ability of at least some patrilineal descendants from passing along Indian status. The restriction was reversed in 1985, however, when amendments to the Indian Act made it possible for this cohort to confer Indian status past the age of 21 under section 6(1)(c), a step that the appeal court regarded as having enhanced the rights of this particular subset of individuals beyond their previous entitlement.[8]

Based on this comparison, the appeal court took exception to the remedy granted at trial. It claimed that the inequality created by the Indian Act was not as expansive or vast in scope as the trial court had maintained. Rather, it was limited only to those impacted by the double mother rule, specifically the superior benefit granted to them as individuals when, following the 1985 amendments, they were able to confer Indian status after the age of 21 under section 6(1)(c). Therefore, the disputed inequality was not, in the eyes of the appeal court, one that involved all "matrilineal and patrilineal descendants," as Justice Ross had initially proposed. Rather, those affected were identified as (1) Jacob Grismer and those registered post-1985 under section 6(1)(c) and (2) those whose status as Indians was preserved under section

6(1)(a) of the 1985 amendments because, and only because, they were the descendants of male Indians.

This is perhaps one of the most confusing aspects of the BC Court of Appeal judgment, but a close reading suggests that, at least in part, the court was answering a call on behalf of the Crown, as the defendant, to have the court acknowledge that no one received a superior benefit in law because of the 1985 amendments. In fact, at trial, the Crown argued that the descendants of male Indians had not acquired Indian status; rather, it had merely been confirmed and maintained by the 1985 amendments to the Indian Act.[9] The appeal court took exception with this argument:

> Sections 6(1)(a) and 6(1)(c) of the *Indian Act* violate the *Charter* to the extent that they grant individuals to whom the Double Mother Rule applied greater rights than they would have had under s. 12(1)(a)(iv) of the former legislation. Accordingly, I would declare ss. 6(1)(a) and 6(1)(c) to be of no force and effect, pursuant to s. 52 of the Constitution Act, 1982.[10]

Whereas the trial court had ordered an expansive judicial remedy to these matters of discrimination by striking down section 6 altogether, the appeal court was narrower in its judgment. It suspended the declaration issued by Justice Ross, granting Parliament twelve months to find a legislative and parliamentary solution to the problem the court itself had delimited.

The *McIvor* case did not end with the BC Court of Appeal decision. Following the consensus judgment issued by Justices Groberman, Newbury, and Tysoe, McIvor sought leave to appeal from the Supreme Court of Canada on June 4, 2009. The appeal was dismissed on November 5, 2009. It can be assumed that the highest court of the land agreed with, or saw no error in the judgment of, the BC Court of Appeal. For its part, Canada introduced Bill C-3, and the Gender Equity in Indian Registration Act received royal assent into law on December 15, 2010.

AS WAS THE CASE with the 1985 amendments to the Indian Act, Status Indians regarded the new legislation with skepticism, even though it restored the rights of those affected by sex discriminatory policy (that is, women, their children, and their grandchildren). In addition to only suspending the two-generation cut off to the third generation, the Gender Equity in Indian Registration Act had other problems. As ha dih nyoh lawyer and activist Mary Eberts (2010, 41) noted, the children of intermarriage "cannot actually invoke the new section to upgrade their registration status from section 6(2) to section 6(1) unless they have a child by birth or adoption" (see also Canadian Bar Association 2010, 5). In effect, the children of women who married non-Indians were still not being treated fairly in relation to the law when compared to their cousins descended through the male line, who have always been registered under section 6(1). In order for Jacob Grismer to be "upgraded" in status – in fact for any child of an out-marrying woman to become a section 6(1) Indian – he or she must have children because "it is the birth of a grandchild which triggers the operation of the proposed new section" (Eberts 2010, 41). This part of the new legislation was not only troublesome in light of the history of institutionalized heterosexism, it was also puzzling (Cannon 1998; Smith 2006).

The new legislation also did nothing to answer the call of Status Indian organizations for the restoration of jurisdiction where governance and citizenship are concerned. The Indigenous Bar Association (2010) raised these precise concerns, noting Canada's duty to consult with Status Indians and its failure to address the issue of jurisdiction. But following the legislation, federal policy makers failed to recognize, affirm, or provide dollars to support Indian political organizations that opposed and challenged the idea of Indian status and the Indian Act altogether and wished to implement their own citizenship laws (*Anishinabek News* 2018a, 2018b). These efforts to restore jurisdiction over citizenship began well before the legislation. Indeed, the Union of Ontario Indians held a conference titled "E-Dbendaagzijig (Those Who Belong)" in the spring of 2007 and launched what it called its Citizenship Law Initiative in June 2008 (*Anishinabek News* 2008). The purpose of both initiatives was to rejuvenate, restore, and have acknowledged Indigenous peoples' inherent right to self-definition. Raising awareness about citizenship law involves rejuvenating and formalizing an understanding of identity and belonging based on real or assumed bonds between people, their shared knowledge of traditional stories or treaty histories, common beliefs, and a tie to some specific territory or place (Cannon 2009; Palmater 2011; Schouls 2003). By focusing on these and other dimensions of belonging, the Union of Ontario Indians drew attention to a history of sovereignty, land, and identity that existed outside of federal legislation (Cannon 2009).

But this does not mean that Canada was prepared to acknowledge the collective identities of Indigenous nations beyond the racialized categories it itself had imposed. *McIvor* was flawed in that it never moved beyond the concept of Indianness, which was clearly a non-negotiable matter in this case. Nor did the case bring policies concerned with Indianness closer in line with the legal parlance of Canadian constitutional law; racialization was not regarded as an analogous form of discrimination under section 15 of the Charter. The courts did not see the Indian Act as discriminating on the basis of sex and race, let alone as legally institutionalizing a distinctly racialized and patriarchal way of thinking about gender, identity, legitimacy, nationhood, family and, indeed, "non-Indian" people and spouses. Instead, Indianness was raised in the case as a commonsense (if not taken-for-granted) category of legal difference, and it was discussed in twelve different paragraphs of the judgment in the context and confines of something loosely referred to by the court as "cultural identity."

According to Justice Ross, Indian status was not merely a legislative category; rather, it was something that had come to make a difference in terms of people's self-concept and their sense of belonging. The court acknowledged the experience of McIvor's son:

> Jacob deposed that while he was growing up he was hurt to be treated as if he was not a "real Indian" by members of the Aboriginal community because he did not have status. He believed that he was a "real Indian," but the exclusion caused him to doubt who he was and to make him feel as if he did not belong anywhere. He felt inferior to his cousins who had Indian status, and felt like an outsider in his own family.[11]

Earlier in the judgment, Ross noted: "Jacob deposed that he was excluded from the annual all Native hockey tournament because he did not have Indian status. He was allowed to play only in his senior year, when his mother acquired status. The students whose parents were Status Indians received funding for their registration fees in athletic activities. Jacob's parents had to pay these fees, at some struggle."[12]

The trial court was unwavering on this point of Indian policy and legislation, noting that "the intangible aspects of status relate to a sense of cultural identity."[13] As Justice Ross further elaborated:

> In my view, status under the *Indian Act* is a concept that is closely akin to the concepts of nationality and citizenship. Status under the *Indian Act*, like citizenship, is governed by statute. The eligibility of a child in both cases is

related to the circumstances of his or her parents. In my
view, the eligibility of the child to registration as an Indian based upon the circumstances of the parent, is a
benefit of the law in which both the parent and the child
have a legitimate interest.[14]

The reasoning of Justice Ross is significant, not only because
it conflates Indian status with culture but also because of the
motivation behind it.

To fully appreciate what was being said, Ross's reasoning
must be read in the context of the case itself, most notably
where it stands in relation to arguments made by the Crown.
A close reading of the reasoning suggests that our status as
Indians might have been looked upon as a mere statutory
classification and nothing more. In fact, the defendants argued that the plaintiffs, Sharon McIvor and Jacob Grismer,
had suffered no discrimination at all, even in light of centuries
of sexism that had prevented women from conferring Indian
status on their descendants. In the eyes of the Crown, Indianness did not confer a benefit under the law, nor was it a thing
of cultural value. The defendants reasoned: "The plaintiffs
suffered no injury. The only difference between the plaintiffs
and Indians entitled to registration pursuant to s. 6(1)(a) of
the 1985 Act is in relation to the status of their children. There
is no right to transmit Indian status, which is purely a matter
of statute. Accordingly, there has been no denial of the plaintiffs' rights."[15]

The trial court took exception to this argument, arguing
to the contrary that Indian status had come to take on a quite
personal if not familial dimension for Status Indians. As
Justice Ross explained:

The defendants' approach would treat status as an Indian
as if it were simply a statutory definition pertaining to
eligibility for some program or benefit. However, having

created and then imposed this identity upon First Nations peoples, with the result that it has become a central aspect of identity, the government cannot now treat it in that way, ignoring the true essence or significance of the concept.[16]

The reasoning reveals what was required to circumscribe the defendant's argument that Indian status holds no meaning at all to Status Indians. At the same time, it also shows how intractable and immune the category "Indian" had become by the twenty-first century. The trial court in no way questioned, or sought to find reparations for, Canada's role in institutionalizing a racialized and notably sexist way of thinking about and understanding Indigenous peoples' identity, lineage, citizenship, governance, and nationhood.

It is true that racialization has required us as nations and individuals to care about our federal recognition as Indians. It is also true that Indianness, regardless of how meaningful it has become, is a colonial-inspired designation that has always been undesirable to us as sovereign nations. In fact, Bonita Lawrence (2004), in *"Real" Indians and Others,* discusses this particular dimension of the Indian Act, highlighting the complex, if not paradoxical, ways in which the category "Indian" operates when it comes to cultural identity. While she does not deny that legal categories shape people's lives in terms of both belonging and identity, she also observes that they "set the terms that individuals must utilize, even in resisting these categories" (Lawrence 2004, 230). *McIvor* did nothing to address or disrupt the fact that, in Canada, Indigenous peoples are still expected to appropriate and work within the confines of Indianness. Nor did it address that it is perhaps preferable to have Canada restore jurisdiction over citizenship to Indigenous nations instead of litigating the matter of Indianness as a cultural identity in Canadian courts of law.

It is unclear why the issue of racialization did not become a central, if not a major, factor in *McIvor*. Indeed, the trial judgment acknowledged the host of identities that stand outside of federal legislation where matters of belonging and citizenship are concerned:

> Despite the imposition of the *Indian Act* regimes, the original First Nations concepts of identity have survived and remain a powerful source of cultural identity. This is vividly illustrated both in the testimony of Ms. McIvor and that of many of those who testified before the Standing Committee. As but one example, [name] testified before the Standing Committee on September 9, 1982, that her real name is [traditional name]. She is from the [name in language] Nation, a member of the [noted] Clan. She regards herself as a member of the [name in language] Nation.[17]

As these testimonies suggest, there are, and have always been, ways of thinking about our identity as Indigenous peoples outside of the Indian Act.

The trial court acknowledged these traditions and went even further by recognizing that Indianness is something that was imposed on us by Canada through federal legislation. As Justice Ross explained:

> The *Royal Commission Report* at c. 2, p. 23 stated that, "the *Indian Act* has created a legal fiction as to cultural identity." The reference to legal fiction is, in my respectful view, an apt reminder of the fact that the concept did not emanate from the Aboriginal people, but was an artificial construct created by the colonists and imposed upon the Aboriginal people. However, the description of the concept as a fiction should not be taken to suggest that the concept lacks meaning or substance. On the contrary, [it] is evident from

the testimony of Sharon and Jacob McIvor, and from that given before the Standing Committee, that this legal fiction has become an important aspect of cultural identity.[18]

While worthy of recognition, this statement stopped short of admitting any wrongdoing on behalf of Canada in creating and then imposing the category "Indian." Furthermore, racialization was not seen as being in any way related to, or for that matter accomplished through, sexism. Nor did the trial court weigh in on the right of Parliament to determine the citizenry of Indigenous peoples through the concept of Indianness and other racialized ways of thinking and knowing.

In refusing to address historical developments, the trial court left the issue of racialization untouched. This demonstrates how, in the case law involving Indian status, the history of racialization can be at once acknowledged and left unaddressed. The court seemed content to conclude that Indianness represented a significant cultural identity; it never moved towards a discussion of jurisdiction. The effect was to render the discrimination faced by Sharon McIvor and her son as being rooted only in sexism. It was as if McIvor was not an Indian, let alone seeking to overcome the inequality that her male child had experienced because of sexism and racism.

THE BC COURT OF APPEAL revisited, and simultaneously avoided, matters of Indianness when it contemplated the case in light of sections 28 and 35 of the Charter. The plaintiffs argued that the Indian Act, in having treated Indian women (along with their male and female descendants) and men differently, had violated their guarantee of equality under section 15 and, indeed, the guarantee of equality to all male and female persons under section 28. Indian women's equality rights were also protected, they reasoned, by section 35(4), which guarantees equality to all male and female "Aboriginal persons." In what amounted to a refusal on behalf of the court to address the issue of racialization and how it was tied intimately to the history of sexism, the appeal court determined that it had neither the "reasoned argument" nor the "evidentiary foundation" before it to consider the question of Indianness. Justice Groberman stated:

> I do not doubt that arguments might be made to the effect that elements of Indian status should be viewed as aboriginal or treaty rights. The interplay between statutory rights of Indians and constitutionally protected aboriginal rights is a complex matter that has not, to date, been thoroughly canvassed in the case law. *It seems likely that, at least for some purposes, Parliament's ability to determine who is and who is not an Indian is circumscribed.* Arguments of this sort, however, have not been addressed in this case. We have neither an evidentiary foundation nor reasoned argument as to the extent to which Indian status should be seen as an aboriginal right rather than a matter for statutory enactment. This case, in short, has not been presented in such a manner as to properly raise issues under s. 35 of the *Constitution Act, 1982*.[19]

It is worth contemplating the sorts of reasoned argument or evidentiary foundation that the appeal court might have wanted to see. It is bewildering that the court did not see McIvor and Grismer (as Indians, after all) as the embodiment of a history that had culminated in invidious distinctions being made between men and women – and, indeed, among Indian men because of their mothers' gender and intermarriage. Indeed, there is a legal argument embedded in *McIvor* in relation to section 35, but it cannot be addressed until the courts start seeing Indigenous women as both Indians and women. Furthermore, the courts must acknowledge that Indian women have faced not only sexism in their own communities but also racialized injustice.

Had the BC Court of Appeal acknowledged this history in *McIvor*, it would have had to consider a set of equally urgent and critical questions related to jurisdiction, including the power that Canada unilaterally designated for itself under section 91(24) of the Constitution Act, 1867. The Indigenous Bar Association outlined the legal argument to be made with respect to acknowledging and affirming Indigenous citizenship (including the jurisdiction to define its parameters) as a "right" protected under section 35. The association also considers it the Crown's duty to consult in cases where Indian status and the much broader question of citizenship are concerned:

> The Supreme Court of Canada in *Haida v. British Columbia* made it clear that the Crown owes a duty to consult whenever it has "knowledge, real or constructive, of the potential existence of the Aboriginal right or title and contemplates conduct that might adversely affect it." While the Crown may invoke its authority under section 91(24) of the *Constitution Act*, 1982 to legislate with respect to "Indians and Lands reserved for Indians," this power must be read together with section 35 of the *Constitution Act*, 1982. As such, the power to legislate with respect to First Nations is explicitly qualified by the need for adequate, meaningful consultation that is consistent with the honour of the Crown. (Indigenous Bar Association 2010, 5–6)

At the level of status quo litigation, the Crown's duty to consult on matters of Indian status would invariably stem from the harm that has been done historically to Indigenous nations. This harm was realized through sexism, which placed men in positions of power within our homes and communities. Both arguments were presented, but the BC Court of Appeal considered neither of them substantively.

To emphasize the point I am making with respect to the inseparability of sexism and racialized injustice, it is the Crown's duty to consult given that the Indian Act, and Indian status in particular, infringes on the right of Indigenous people to determine their own membership. The Indigenous Bar Association (2010, 5) expands on this point: "Parliament has been afforded an opportunity to meaningfully recognize and implement systems of membership based on Indigenous legal traditions. By disregarding the opportunity to address their broader issues, the Crown is depriving Indigenous nations of their ability to exercise their aboriginal, treaty, and international rights to govern their own citizens."

The BC Court of Appeal never managed to address these questions about Indigenous citizenship, jurisdiction, and racialization because the court failed to complicate the question of sex discrimination in both its reasoning and judgment. When racialization and sexism are detached from each other, especially in relation to weighing in on issues concerning sections 28 and 35, the outcome is a raceless story of sexism, which prevented the BC Court of Appeal from recognizing the unequal treatment that Indigenous women and their descendants have faced as Indians in Canada. During the original trial, even Justice Ross, in contemplating these matters, admitted to the court the full complexity of issues that had been presented to her with respect to Indian status and restoring equality to Indian women. In response to the defendant's claim that the plaintiffs did not have a viable claim under section 15 because the Canadian Charter cannot be applied retroactively to repair historical injustices, she reasoned:

> Strictly speaking, it is correct to say that the only way to give absolutely equal treatment to all persons would be to either grant status to spouses of Indian women who, prior to April 17, 1985, married persons who were not Status Indians, or to take away the status of the women

who married Status Indians prior to April 17, 1985, and acquired status from their husbands. However, the plain-tiffs do not seek any relief in relation to the non-Indian spouses of Status Indians. That is, the plaintiffs do not seek equal treatment with respect to the non-Indian spouses of Indians, either in the form of granting or removing status. Rather, they seek treatment for Indian women and their children who claim Indian descent through them that is equal to that afforded to Indian men and their descend-ants. The defendants' submission overlooks the provisions of earlier versions of the Indian Act that granted registra-tion status to the legitimate child of a male person who was registered or entitled to be registered as an Indian, for example, s. 11(d) of the 1951 Act.[20]

The BC Court of Appeal stumbled through the matter of "ab-solute equal treatment," deciding in the end that McIvor's and Grismer's status in relation to non-Indian people was not what either of them were asking the court to address. What the appeal court should have done in *McIvor* to secure justice for women such as McIvor – and, indeed, for Status Indians in general – was broaden the scope of sex discrimination to include all women legally defined as Indians. We will not challenge colonial dominance, Indianness, or a state-based way of thinking about identity, citizenship, and nationhood until this happens. And we will continue to overlook a series of urgent questions about jurisdiction.

There is good reason to be skeptical that Canadian law can resolve colonial grievances or issues of substantive inequality related to Indianness and Indigenous sovereignty. As Colin Samson (1999, 19) argues, colonial law is not concerned with Indigenous sovereignty; rather, it focuses on the infringe-ment of rights and the procedures that colonial governments must follow in order to legally extinguish Aboriginal title. It is through this process of deciding when and how the rights of "Aboriginal peoples" can be infringed upon that the law accomplishes the ongoing usurpation of lands. Samson refers to this process of colonial law as a "magical contrivance" (23). Through cases such as *McIvor*, Canada reasserts its sovereignty as a settler nation. Courts in general are steadfast in refusing to acknowledge Indigenous peoples as nations or, for that matter, anything beyond Aboriginal title. Ha dih nyoh scholar James Tully (2000, 45) has observed that "the law incorporates Indigenous peoples into Canada and subjects them to the Canadian Constitution in the very act of recognizing their rights as rights within the Canadian Constitution." This tautological move protects Canadian sovereignty, as does foreclosing examinations of the concept of Indianness in Canadian law. The courts' consideration of sex discrimination in the Indian Act therefore enables Canada to avoid addressing its colonial existence (P. Monture 2006).

As a settler colony, Canada is unwilling to acknowledge the sovereignty of Indigenous peoples, including our ability to claim jurisdiction over our own identity and citizenship. There has been no federal acknowledgment of our identity and citizenship as nations based on our conceptions of belonging, our original treaties, or our nation-to-nation agreements. Although we did not relinquish our sovereignty at contact, nor our ability to determine and identify who it is that belongs to our nations as citizens, Canadian law has tended to disregard, if not actively work to supplant through legislation, these identities and practices. It has not questioned the myth of settler sovereignty and how it is connected to the process of outside naming. Even the use and occupation of our traditional lands has been reduced to the issue of "Aboriginal title," a designation created by the law to address what ought to be considered a recolonizing move.

Before we can hope to achieve justice, the matter of recolonization – that is, the process whereby Indigenous peoples

are subsumed by a legal apparatus that serves settler interests – needs to be addressed. We need to question how our
sovereign right to exercise jurisdiction over our lands and territories – and most fundamentally, our own identities and
the naming of our people – has been reduced to the issue of
rights and rights infringement. It is incumbent upon Canadian
courts and Parliament, as well as Canadian citizens, to understand that there would be no such thing as Indians or Indian
reserves – or any other lands that exist in what is now called
Canada – without the undermining of treaty and nation-to-
nation agreements as well as various racialization processes
and strategies of usurpation.

The racialization we are challenging today is tied as much
to white settler colonialism as it is to Indianness. We are asking that "Indian" be questioned as an antiquated designation that has worked to secure settler sovereignty. Many
Status Indians are challenging the idea that our identity is
determined by federal legislation. In saying that we are nations
and, furthermore, citizens of these nations, we not only oppose
the Indian Act, we also oppose an identity-making process
that has been – and is still is – fundamental to building
Canada as a nation (Thobani 2007). In resisting the category
"Indian," we ask Canadians to think about the role that the
Indian Act has played in the creation and proliferation of
colonial settlements and, indeed, in creating lands for the
taking. We are saying that Indianness has played a significant
role in who settlers understand themselves to be and that our
territories extend far beyond those assigned to us through
identity-classification schemes.

Courts and Parliament have been slow to answer pointed
and outward calls to address the issues of sovereignty, outside naming, Indigenous citizenship, self-definition, and settler colonialism. Canada regards Indian status injustices as
best (re)solved through amendments to the Indian Act. In

order to achieve true justice for Indigenous peoples, Canada must literally undertake the impossible. It must acknowledge identities that exist outside of the federal legislation it created to appropriate and dispossess us of lands. It must rejuvenate its own treaty and nation-to-nation agreements in partnership with Indigenous allies. It must acknowledge that the theft of lands was accomplished through the doctrine of Indianness. Furthermore, it must relinquish and move beyond the power it granted itself under section 91(24) of the Constitution Act.

Conclusion

A RECURRENT TENDENCY in the case law and politics surrounding Indian status has been to compartmentalize and treat histories of sexism and racialization as if they were fundamentally unrelated. In politics, the tendency has been to frame "women's rights" as "individual rights" – as if they existed apart from, or even in opposition to, the rights that belong to "Indians" or the Status Indian collective. As I have shown throughout this book, not only are these histories related, the relationship between them, including the racialized processes whereby we became "Indians" for state administrative purposes and the dispossession of lands, has often been marginalized or disregarded entirely. The effect has been to distort the historical record to such a degree that the discrimination experienced by some Indigenous peoples has been linked to their categorization as "women" or "Indians" but never both. This way of thinking is unproductive. Over the past four decades, it has detracted attention away from the degree to which we have all been impacted by sexism – as Indians, and as men and women. It has stood in the way of realizing a politics of recognition and citizenship that can overturn the effects of racist patriarchy. But what are the implications of this realization in terms of reimagining Indigenous identity and citizenship in Canada?

My nation, the Six Nations, are matrilineal, meaning that we trace our ancestry through our (grand)mothers. Many of us wish to retain this matrilineal way of thinking in our hearts and minds. Although the Indian Act has reversed and denigrated the idea of women's power and knowledge, we have not forgotten. It is difficult to envisage our survival as nations without first coming to grips with our (grand)mothers' attempts to combat patriarchy. Their grievances were acts of resurgence and regeneration, not simply demands for gender equality. Indeed, their knowledge and actions provide the very basis upon which we can begin to imagine and (re)create a new and different future, especially where matters of identity and citizenship are concerned. And this knowledge needs to be acknowledged by Canadian law as the foundation for how we have done our kinship business for centuries.

Canada needs to acknowledge who we are as Indigenous peoples and citizens outside of federal jurisdiction and colonial legislation. As an inseparable part of this process, Indigenous people need to understand how we belong outside of racialized ways of thinking. Indigenous ways of knowing our kin relations must be rejuvenated and then acknowledged and affirmed by the courts. Rob Porter (1998), a Seneca scholar, has written of kinship and the impact of "Americanization" on Haudenosaunee peoples. Following Laurence M. Hauptman (1988), he defines Americanization as a series of policy objectives concerned with our assimilation and annihilation as peoples (Porter 1998, 826n79). More importantly, following Russel L. Barsh (1993), he sees it as an all-enveloping set of attitudes that have pervaded our existence and thinking as Haudenosaunee peoples. We have become increasingly concerned with corporate capitalist exploitation, individualism, and monetary gain, and our communities have increasingly been weakened by dysfunction, defensiveness, and a culture of mistrust (Porter 1998, 910–11n424). Porter warns that "our end will come when we no longer have or desire kinship with one another" (Porter 1998, 931n451).

If this is true, then we need to recognize the urgency of linking sexism to attacks on kinship organization and our disempowerment as peoples (see Sunseri 2011). Our existence as nations flows from all our female relations. We need to understand and talk pointedly about the complex vagaries of colonialism, sexism, and racialization, especially the way they have placed men and women into an unequal relationship with each other as "Indians." It is at this precise juncture of decolonization and legal transformation that men must come to unequivocally understand and speak out about sexism and how it has impacted our lives as Indians. The rights of Indian women and children cannot be delimited to individuals. As I have shown, the rights of women do not only belong to women as individuals – they belong to all of us.

IT IS PERHAPS reassuring to know that the politics of Indian status have started to change in the twenty-first century. Injustices are increasingly understood as the outcome of gender and race discrimination. In part, this new politics of citizenship and identity has followed on the heels of demographic changes, including the ongoing legal assimilation of registered or Status Indians (Clatworthy 2003a, 2003b; M. Mann 2005). It is perhaps also reassuring to know that there are fewer reasons to oppose women who are challenging sexism today than there were in the 1970s. Aboriginal title to the land has become part of Canadian law, so Indigenous organizations no longer fear the extinguishment of title or stage their opposition to women's rights on this basis (Turner 2006, 2013; Jamieson 1978).

When the Canadian government initiated an "exploratory process" to examine issues of Indian status and citizenship following criticisms of the 2010 Gender Equity in Indian

Registration Act (Aboriginal Affairs and Northern Development Canada 2011), fifty-five national, regional, and local organizations participated in the process. Among the recommendations made in its final report were calls for "the recognition of First Nations rights to determine who is eligible to be registered as an Indian and a member of an Indian Band; the elimination of all residual gender-based inequalities and categories of Indians under section 6, including the second-generation cut-off; [and] addressing issues related to unstated paternity, adoption and status Indians without Canadian citizenship or permanent residency." The report also noted that First Nations participants held an unanimously "high expectation" that "the federal government will move forward on reforms in respect of the *Indian Act* in the shorter-term, with the recognition and implementation of First Nations jurisdiction over citizenship as a medium to longer-term goal" (Indigenous and Northern Affairs Canada 2013). The recommendations were a significant development, particularly since Canada, as of May 10, 2016, is a signatory to the United Nations Declaration on the Rights of Indigenous Peoples (UNDRIP).

International forums, legal instruments, and courts are increasingly becoming a viable route for addressing historical injustices involving Indian status and citizenship. There has been a global effort to recognize and affirm the collective rights of Indigenous peoples as flowing from elderly women and "the force of matrilineal ties" (Fiske and George 2006, 65), which is, I believe, the key to resolving some of the historical grievances related to sexism and Indianness. Sharon McIvor has asked the United Nations Human Rights Committee to consider upholding the trial court's decision in *McIvor v The Registrar, Indian and Northern Affairs Canada*.[1] In her petition, she asked that the descendants of Indian women be placed on the same footing as those of Indian men in terms of being able to confer Indian status.[2] The appeal itself is an important and necessary step in drawing international attention to Indian status and citizenship injustices in Canada.

If the UN rules favourably on McIvor's behalf, we can expect to see further amendments to the Indian Act, which would represent a legal victory for federally recognized peoples in Canada. However, it will not bring about justice if the discussion about sexism is divorced from a discussion of racialization or Indianness. UNDRIP represents a new option for challenging the Indian Act because it offers a vehicle to repudiate the doctrine of discovery upon which Canada is premised as a settler state (see Cannon and Sunseri 2011, 273; Manuel and Derrickson 2017; R.J. Miller et al. 2010; Trask 2002; Trask 2003, 36–37). It acknowledges Indigenous sovereignty and contests the idea of terra nullius. Article 26(2) states: "Indigenous peoples have the right to own, use, develop and control the lands, territories and resources that they possess *by reason of traditional ownership or other traditional occupation or use,* as well as those which they have otherwise acquired."[3] Article 27 outlines the role of the state:

> States shall establish and implement, in conjunction with indigenous peoples concerned, a fair, independent, impartial, open and transparent process, giving due recognition to indigenous peoples' laws, traditions, customs and land tenure systems, to recognize and adjudicate the rights of indigenous peoples pertaining to their lands, territories and resources, *including those which were traditionally owned or otherwise occupied or used. Indigenous peoples shall have the right to participate in this process.*[4]

Articles 26 and 27 set out a standard for thinking about and affirming the existence of Indigenous sovereignty, legal traditions, and the ancient and epic philosophical legacies that surround them, including philosophies that relate to land, belonging, and identity. UNDRIP affirms that Indigenous peoples are not simply racialized minorities, they are original peoples. They are unique, complex, and possess *sui generis* (one of a kind) sovereignty as nations under the law (Henderson 2002).

The relationship we hold as Indigenous peoples with Canada stems not from the Indian Act or Indian policy: it stems from our shared history as sovereign nations who came together as allies and partners (see Fleras 2009, 78). Our relationship with Canada should not be based on a legal system that requires us to "prove" that our "traditions" are static and unchanging (Luk 2009–10). We need to challenge Canada on its right to assume jurisdiction where determining our citizenship is concerned. Article 33 of UNDRIP holds that

(1) Indigenous peoples have the right to determine their own identity or membership in accordance with their customs and traditions. This does not impair the right of indigenous individuals to obtain citizenship of the States in which they live.

(2) Indigenous peoples have the right to determine the structures and to select the membership of their institutions in accordance with their own procedures.

Thus, we have a right as Indigenous nations to decide who our citizens are. We have a right as nations to decide who belongs. Most of all, we have the right to reject – or outwardly resign from – racialized and patriarchal ways of thinking.

We should embrace article 33 – but only if the language of rights is rejected, and only if the politics of recognition becomes more focused on the racialized damage caused by sexism. The idea of rights, as discussed, carries a great deal of baggage. The law would have us believe that colonial grievances can be resolved through human rights discourse. But the law is seductive. We utilize its terms to achieve small concessions for the colonial injustices we have faced as Indigenous peoples. Sometimes we win, but these victories have only been within the realm of status quo litigation. Some major victories have taken place over the past four decades in terms of sexism, but we have yet to witness a case that connects sexism to Indianness. Nor has Canada done anything to restore jurisdiction over citizenship to Indigenous peoples. These matters require the attention of the international courts, but there is also a great deal of work to be done at home.

Audra Simpson, for instance, has developed the concept of feeling citizenship to challenge the legacies of racialization and sexism. *Feeling citizenship* refers to "an affective sense of being Mohawk of Kanawà:ke, in spite of the lack of recognition that some might unjustly experience" (Simpson 2014, 173–74). Feeling citizenship frees us from alternative conceptions of identity rooted in laws established by the settler state. Ojibwe/Dakota scholar Scott Lyons (2010, 37, 40) likewise suggests that we focus on the everyday social processes that create our identities intersubjectively, that we need to think about Indianness less as a thing and instead as something that is created through the things that we do together. Both Simpson and Lyons suggest that identity and belonging extend well beyond the state and its restrictive regime of Indianness. At the same time, they do not deny how the history of racialization has framed our lives as Indians.

Notwithstanding the fact that the law represents a double-edged sword for Indigenous peoples, we should consider having racialization acknowledged as an analogous form of discrimination under the Canadian Charter of Rights and Freedoms. Historically, *race* and *racialization* have meant two different things. *Race* refers to a social construction without any basis in biological reality (Henry and Tator 2006). *Racialization* is the process through which race takes on its material significance. Racialization is not listed as enumerated grounds for discrimination under the Charter, but this does not mean that it has not, as a form of discrimination, wreaked havoc on our communities. It is a form of discrimination analogous to that of the enumerated grounds listed under section 15 of the Charter – namely, "race, national or ethnic origin, colour, religion, sex, age or mental or physical disability."

In the 1990s, Status Indians witnessed a significant victory where the matter of analogous discrimination is concerned. As discussed, the Corbiere decision confirmed that off-reserve residents have a vested interest, and a right to participate, in band council elections. The Supreme Court of Canada decided that Status Indians could not exclude off-reserve members from the election of band council governments and that "aboriginality-residence" constituted an analogous form of discrimination under section 15 of the Charter. The judgment suggests that the courts are willing to reverse forms of discrimination rooted in the Indian Act, including sexism. Through its judgment, the court recognized the history of wrongdoing where involuntary enfranchisement is concerned. The same should be done about racialization.

We need to challenge the Indian Act as a piece of colonial legislation that has – for too long – required us to think in racialized terms about ourselves and others. We need to show that the Indian Act institutionalized a category of race that was used to place Indigenous women into an unequal relationship with Indigenous men and also in relation to settler women. Federal legislation made "Indians" out of white women. It also required the idea of "woman follows man" to take on new significance and meaning in Indigenous communities. While some might argue that my analysis is overly deterministic, I conclude by restating that although Indigenous peoples may have the discretionary choice to identify as nations, this does not mean that Canada is prepared to recognize them. Nor does it mean that a fiduciary obligation will be seen to exist between Canada and those it deems "non-Indians" under the law (Cannon 2008, 12).

THAT HISTORICAL INJUSTICES are far from being resolved became clear when Stéphane Descheneaux's case came before the courts in 2015. Like *McIvor*, the *Descheneaux* case addressed the matter of residual sex discrimination in section 6 of the Indian Act. Descheneaux, of the Abénaki of Odanak First Nation of Quebec, had three children who could not register as Indians because of their great-grandmother's gender and intermarriage. His case was heard by the Superior Court of Quebec along with fellow plaintiffs Susan and Tammy Yantha, a mother and daughter impacted by Canada's policy concerning paternity and those born out of wedlock.[5] Together, they argued that "s. 6 of the *Indian Act* violates the equality guaranteed in 15(1) of the *Canadian Charter of Rights and Freedoms* by creating discriminatory and differential treatment in regards to who is or is not a Status Indian" (Indigenous Bar Association 2017, 9). In hearing the case, Justice Chantal Masse ruled in favour of the plaintiffs and on August 3, 2015, declared: "Paragraphs 6(1)(a), (c) and (f) and subsection 6(2) of the Indian Act unjustifiably infringe section 15 of the *Canadian Charter of Rights and Freedoms* and are inoperative."[6] She suspended the declaration of invalidity until February 3, 2017, a period of eighteen months, to give Canada the time to remedy the discrimination.[7]

Canada responded with Bill S-3, An Act to Amend the Indian Act, in October 2016 (Indigenous and Northern Affairs Canada 2017). The bill was part of a two-stage plan to address sexism in the Indian Act. The first stage would eliminate "known sex-based inequities in Indian registration" through legislative amendments. Bill S-3 reached a Senate Standing Committee in November 2016. After lengthy discussions – and after hearing from numerous organizations and witnesses – the Senate voted unanimously to pass an amended version of the bill to ameliorate the effects of other and "more complex" sources of sex discrimination in the Indian Act going all the way back to the nineteenth century (Indigenous Bar Association 2017, 2; Galloway 2017a). The Senate's recommendation was dubbed "the s.6(1)(a) all the way remedy" (Canada 2017, 6, 7). Canada rejected the amendments, promising further consultations in the second stage, once Bill S-3 was passed into law. It cited fears about an increase in the Status Indian population if status were restored to Indigenous women who had married non-Indigenous men prior to 1951 (Canadian Bar Association 2016, 7). In January 2017, having run out of time and with calls by the Senate to amend the bill, Canada sought and gained a five-month extension.

In the back and forth between the House of Commons and the Senate, it became clear that Canada was willing to amend the Indian Act, but only in ways that addressed the discrimination facing Status Indians in precisely the same circumstances as Stéphane Descheneaux, Susan Yantha, and Tammy Yantha. The bill finally passed into law and took effect on December 12, 2017, but the law to date has refused to follow "the s.6(1)(a) all the way remedy" recommended by the Canadian Senate (NWAC 2018b, 16). There are other problems with what has come to be known as An Act to Amend the Indian Act in Response to the Superior Court of Quebec Decision in Descheneaux c. Canada (Procureur général). A hierarchy of status remains in place between the 6(1)(a) (male category) and 6(1)(c) (reinstated female category), whereby "women and their descendants are relegated to a different, often stigmatized and deemed 'lesser' category of status" (NWAC 2018a, 1). The matters of unstated paternity (where Indigenous women must still provide "evidence" of paternity when that information is either impossible to acquire or traumatizing) and band membership (where women can still experience discrimination from their own communities) have also yet to be reconciled (NWAC 2018a, 2). The situation in general has led Indigenous women's organizations (and some men) to call on Ottawa to demand an end to sex discrimination (Lamirande 2019).

Descheneaux and Bill S-3 have both garnered a great deal of attention in Canadian newspapers, especially among those critical of the Trudeau Liberals' "commitment to reconciliation and a renewed nation-to-nation relationship with Indigenous peoples" (Indigenous and Northern Affairs Canada 2017). The government's response to the Senate's amendments, however, has made it clear that the Canadian government is still not in the business of addressing substantive matters of land, racialization in the first historical instance of Indianness, or Indigenous nationhood – nor is it in the business of making any more Indians.

It is clear that Canada continues to be caught up in a politics of recognition that invites a settler colonial and highly racialized way of thinking about equality, identity, and belonging. As the Indigenous Bar Association (2017, 30) suggests, it is now time to move beyond constructions that keep us trapped in a conversation about how to make the Indian Act more just or "fair" and to start thinking about the restoration of jurisdiction. Indeed, the association recommended that

Bill S-3 be amended to contemplate the formation of an independent panel with the mandate to research, consult and report on the next steps for implementing Indigenous jurisdiction over membership, including a mandate to make recommendations for the elimination of Indian status system in favour of an approach which advances Indigenous sovereignty and is consistent with the federal government's responsibilities for Indians under section 91(24). (Indigenous Bar Association 2017, 33)

The very notion of Indianness and the Indian Act will need to be challenged. On this point, Gerald Taiaiake Alfred (2005,

165) writes: "Freedom from colonization is the sense of an unbounded self and the ability to live fully in a wide and open world. It is to feel and live large! Being 'Indian' and being 'aboriginal' is accepting a small self, imprisonment in the small space created for us by the white man: reserves, aboriginal rights, Indian Act entitlements, etc."

John Borrows (2008, 11–31), an Anishinaabe scholar, suggests that we look towards home to put an end to the Indian Act. The power to dismantle its hold over us as nations resides not only in litigation but also in recognizing how fundamentally opposed the Indian Act stands in relation to what is known of our traditional understandings of the good life. We can, he argues, put an end to the Indian Act if we apply seven principles intended to animate our lives as Indigenous peoples:

Wisdom Use our language and spirituality to inform educational initiatives (formal and informal), including the reduction of community-based violence and addictions.

Love Return to values and principles that work to revitalize and promote familial relations, extended kinship belonging, and communal participation.

Respect Extend and realize a caring, compassionate, and selfless way of living respectfully together in reserve-based communities.

Bravery Work with the Crown and Canada to realize different or new sorts of relationships based on partnerships instead of subjugation.

Humility Be mindful of our strengths, limits, and weaknesses when striving to reinvent or change our circumstances as individuals and peoples.

Honesty Broaden our understanding of what it means to be an Indigenous person in terms of spirituality, resources, relationships, participation, and residency.

Truth   Recognize that our existence does not stem from
our "race" but from our status as political groups
who share ongoing, historical (inter)relationships.

We cannot look only to litigation in international forums to
resolve colonial grievances – much less to put an end to the
Indian Act. As Borrows suggests, we need to re(centre) and
follow principles of governance that have their origins in the
good life, including Indigenous legal traditions (Borrows 2010).
We must revisit and think more about our own systems of
knowledge. This means looking to stories about our roles and
responsibilities as men and women and stories about gender
balance and complementarity. Just as the Creation Story and
Great Law are significant to the Haudenosaunee, living the
"good life" is central to Anishinaabe relations. The Indian Act
loses its effectiveness when this type of revitalization takes place
(Borrows 2010, 31). Of course, these practices will mean nothing at home until putting an end to racist patriarchy is seen as
an integral and inseparable part of the decolonizing process.

At some critical point we will need to contemplate the
work that needs to be done to dismantle Indian Act patriarchy.
Finding a way out of the Indian Act cannot take place until
we give critical thought to sexism, its impact on our communities, and its impact on men; until we think about the
responsibility we have as men to refuse its parameters. We
will surely come up short in seeking to liberate ourselves from
colonialism if we maintain a relationship of sexism between
Indian men and women. We need to redefine what it means
to be a part of sexism as Indigenous peoples in Canada. We
especially need to think about what it might look like to resign, practically and theoretically, from it. If sexism relies on
Indian men to affirm, initiate, and corroborate its power, then
it is clearly time for our resignation. It is time to contemplate
a new series of masculinities realized under an antisexist and
anticolonial paradigm.

Notes

Introduction

1 Canada, Parliament, House of Commons, *Minutes of Proceedings and Evidence of the Standing Committee on Indian Affairs and Northern Development*, 29th Parl, 1st sess, No 2, February 22, 1973.

2 In Canadian law, the term *Indigenous peoples* comprises First Nations ("Indians"), Inuit, and Métis. Métis refers to an individual or nation of people whose origins emerged historically from the intermarriage of Indigenous women and European men during the fur trade era in Canada. It refers to a current and increasing population of individuals who are defined by their "mixed-ness." *Métis* should not, however, be used as a catch-all phrase for all persons of mixed birth and background, nor should it be used to refer to Indigenous peoples who have been enfranchised or legally excluded from Indianness (Lawrence 2012, 5). As Métis scholar Chris Andersen (2011, 165) argues, *Métis* refers to the "memories, territories, and leaders who challenged and continue to challenge colonial authorities' unitary claims to land and society." It refers to a people of unique ethnocultural ancestry, heritage, and peoplehood.

3 The creation story is drawn from Cannon (2004), Cannon and Sunseri (2017, x–xiii), S. Hill (2017, 20–24), R. Monture (2014, 3), and Sunseri (2011, 15–17).

4 The story of the Great Law of Peace is drawn generally from S. Hill (2017), Porter (1998), Mohawk (1994), and North American Indian Travelling College (1984). The quotes are from Porter (1998, 815) [gift from the Creator]; S. Hill (2017) [great, proper path]; Mohawk (1994) [All order and safety, xvi] [Righteousness means justice, 15]; S. Hill (2017) [cultivators of the soil; lived along the warpath; They shall name the Chiefs, 58] [first Yakoyaner, 59].

5 H. Con. Res 331 (100th Congress), A concurrent resolution to acknowledge the contribution of the Iroquois Confederacy of Nations to the development of the United States Constitution and to reaffirm the continuing government-to-government relationship between Indian tribes and the United States established in the Constitution.

6 While some scholars in Canada have expressed concern about labelling policy, events, and efforts aimed at the elimination of Indigenous peoples "genocidal" (see Palmater 2015, 52–55; Vowell 2016, 174; Woolford, Benvenuto, and Hinton 2014, 2), Canada's Truth and Reconciliation Commission did not hesitate to do so: "For over a century, the central goals of Canada's Aboriginal policy were to eliminate Aboriginal governments; ignore Aboriginal rights; terminate the Treaties; and, through a process of assimilation, cause Aboriginal peoples to cease to exist as distinct legal, social, cultural, religious, and racial entities in Canada. The establishment and operation of residential schools were a central element of this policy, which can best be described as 'cultural genocide'" (quoted in Vowell 2016, 173; see also Truth and Reconciliation Commission of Canada 2015).

Chapter 1: The Indian Act, a Legacy of Racist Patriarchy

1 Indian Act, SC 1895, c 35, s 3. See also Tobias (1983, 46–47).

2 Haudenosaunee Confederacy, "Statement of the Haudenosaunee Concerning the Constitutional Framework and International Position of the Haudenosaunee Confederacy," 1982, in Canada, Parliament, House of Commons, *Minutes of Proceedings and Evidence of the Special Committee on Indian Self-Government,*" 32nd Parl, 1st sess, No 31, June 1, 1983, 12, emphasis mine.

3 Indian Act, SC 1876, c 18 (39 Vict).

4 Indian Act, RSC 1927, c 98; see also Venne 1981, 252.

5 Indian Act, RSC 1951, c 29; see also Venne 1981, 320.

6 Indian Act, SC 1956, c 40, s 12(2).

Chapter 2: Sexism, Racialized Injustice, and *Lavell v Canada,* 1969–73

1 *Lavell v Canada, Attorney General* (1971), 22 DLR (3rd) (Ont Co Ct) at para 184.

2 *Attorney General of Canada v Lavell* and *Isaac v Bédard*, [1974] SCR 1349 [*Lavell-Bédard*].

3 Canada, Parliament, House of Commons, *Minutes of Proceedings and Evidence of the Standing Committee on Indian Affairs and Northern Development*, 29th Parl, 1st sess, No 2, February 22, 1973.

4 Ibid 8, 16.

5 *R v Drybones*, [1970] SCR 282.

6 Indian Act, SC 1970, c 1–6; Venne (1981), 448.

7 *Lavell-Bédard* at para 1372.

8 Ibid at para 1350.

9 Ibid at para 1366.

10 Ibid at paras 1375 and 1383.

11 Ibid at para 1372.

12 Ibid at para 1356.

Chapter 3: Individual versus Collective Rights in Status Indian Politics, 1985–99

1 UN General Assembly, International Covenant on Civil and Political Liberties, December 16, 1966, United Nations, Treaty Series, vol. 999, 171.

2 *Sandra Lovelace v Canada*, Communication No R.6/24, UN Doc Supp No 40 (A/36/40) at 166 (1981), p. 17.

3 Indian Act, RSC 1985, c I-5.

4 *Scrimbett v Sakimay Indian Band Council*, [2000] 1 CNLR 205 at para 71; see also Magnet (2003).

5 Ibid at para 33.

6 *Six Nations of the Grand River Band v Henderson*, [1997] 1 CNLR 202.

7 *Goodswimmer v Canada*, [1994] 2 CNLR 56 at para 3.

8 *Courtois v Canada, Minister of Indian Affairs and Northern Development*, [1991] 1 CNLR 40.

9 *Sawridge Band v Canada*, [1995] 4 CNLR 121 at para 64.

10 *Corbiere v Canada (Minister of Indian and Northern Affairs)*, [1999] 2 SCR 203 at para 8.

11 Ibid at para 19.

12 *Sawridge Band v Canada*, [1996] 1 FC 3.

13 Ibid at para 64.

14 *Sawridge Band v Canada*, [1997] 3 FC 380.

15 *Sawridge Band v Canada,* [1996] 1 FC 3 at para 23.
16 Ibid.
17 *Sawridge Band v Canada,* [1997] 3 FC 380.
18 *Native Women's Association of Canada et al and The Queen; Native Council of Canada et al* (1992) Intervenants 95 DLR 106.
19 Canada, Parliament, House of Commons, *Minutes of Proceedings and Evidence of the Standing Committee on Indian Affairs and Northern Development,* 32nd Parl, 1st sess, No 58, September 21, 1982, 22.
20 Ibid; Mercredi and Turpel (1993).
21 *Gehl v Canada (Attorney General),* [2001] 4 CNLR 108 at para 6.
22 *Gehl* v Canada *(Attorney General),* 2017 ONCA 319.
23 Ibid at para 52.

Chapter 4: Sexism, Indigenous Sovereignty, and *McIvor v The Registrar,* 2007–09

1 *McIvor v The Registrar, Indian and Northern Affairs,* 2007 BCSC 827; Gender Equity in Indian Registration Act, SC 2010, c 18.
2 Canada, Senate of Canada, *Proceedings of the Standing Senate Committee on Human Rights. Issue #8 Second (Final) Meeting on: Bill C-3, an Act to Promote Gender Equity in Indian Registration by Responding to the Court of Appeal for British Columbia Decision in McIvor v Canada (Registrar of Indian and Northern Affairs),* 40th Leg, 3rd sess, December 6, 2010.
3 Ibid.
4 *McIvor v The Registrar, Indian and Northern Affairs,* 2007 BCSC 827 at para 343.
5 Ibid at para 351.
6 *McIvor v The Registrar, Indian and Northern Affairs,* 2009 BCCA 153 at paras 95 and 97.
7 Ibid at para 5.
8 Ibid at para 138.
9 Ibid at para 84.
10 Ibid at para 161.
11 *McIvor v The Registrar, Indian and Northern Affairs,* 2007 BCSC 827 at para 137.
12 Ibid at para 130.
13 Ibid at para 132.
14 Ibid at para 192.

15 Ibid at para 6.
16 Ibid at para 193.
17 Ibid at para 132.
18 Ibid at para 134.
19 *McIvor v The Registrar, Indian and Northern Affairs*, 2009 BCCA 153 at para 66, emphasis mine.
20 *McIvor v The Registrar, Indian and Northern Affairs*, 2007 BCSC 827 at para 236.

Conclusion

1 *Sharon McIvor and Jacob Grismer v Canada*, 2010 at para 75.
2 Ibid at para 247.
3 UN General Assembly, United Nations Declaration on the Rights of Indigenous Peoples: Resolution, adopted by the General Assembly, October 2, 2007, A/RES/61/295, emphasis mine.
4 Ibid, emphasis mine.
5 *Descheneaux v Canada*, 2015 QCCS 3555 at paras 63 and 65.
6 Ibid at paras 228 and 245.
7 Ibid at para 246.

References

Case Law

Attorney General of Canada v Lavell and Isaac v Bédard, [1974] SCR 1349.

Corbiere v Canada (Minister of Indian and Northern Affairs), [1999] 2 SCR 203.

Courtois v Canada, Minister of Indian Affairs and Northern Development, [1991] 1 CNLR 40.

Descheneaux v Canada, 2015 QCCS 3555.

Gehl v Canada (Attorney General), [200l] 4 CNLR 108.

Gehl v Canada (Attorney General), 2017 ONCA 319.

Goodswimmer v Canada, [1994] 2 CNLR 56.

Lavell v Canada, Attorney General (1971), 22 DLR (3rd) (Ont Co Ct).

McIvor v The Registrar, Indian and Northern Affairs, 2007 BCSC 827.

McIvor v The Registrar, Indian and Northern Affairs, 2009 BCCA 153.

Native Women's Association of Canada et al and The Queen; Native Council of Canada et al (1992) Intervenants 95 DLR 106.

R v Drybones, [1970] SCR 282

Sandra Lovelace v Canada, Communication No R.6/24, UN Doc Supp No 40 (A/36/40) at 166 (1981).

Sawridge Band v Canada, [1995] 4 CNLR 121.

Sawridge Band v Canada, [1996] 1 FC 3.

Sawridge Band v Canada, [1997] 3 FC 380.

Scrimbett v Sakimay Indian Band Council, [2000] 1 CNLR 205.

Six Nations of the Grand River Band v Henderson, [1997] 1 CNLR 202.

Other Sources

Aboriginal Affairs and Northern Development Canada. 2011. *Exploratory Process on Indian Registration, Band Membership and Citizenship: An Overview.* Ottawa: Indian and Northern Affairs Canada.

Alfred, Gerald Taiaiake. 1993. "The People." In *Words That Come before All Else: Environmental Philosophies of the Haudenosaunee,* edited by Haudenosaunee Environmental Task Force, 8–14. Cornwall Island, ON: North American Travelling College.

–. 1999. *Peace, Power, Righteousness: An Indigenous Manifesto.* Don Mills, ON: Oxford University Press.

–. 2005. *Wasáse: Indigenous Pathways of Action and Freedom.* Peterborough, ON: Broadview Press.

–. 2014. "Reimagining Warriorhood: A Conversation with Taiaiake Alfred." In *Masculindians: Conversations about Indigenous Manhood,* edited by Sam McKegney, 76–86. Winnipeg: University of Manitoba Press.

Alfred, Gerald Taiaiake, and Jeff Corntassel. 2005. "Being Indigenous: Resurgences against Contemporary Colonialism." *Government and Opposition* 40 (4): 597–614.

Andersen, Chris. 2011. "'I'm Métis, What's Your Excuse?' On the Optics and the Ethics of the Misrecognition of Métis in Canada." *Aboriginal Policy Studies* 1 (2): 161–65.

–. 2014. *Métis: Race, Recognition, and the Struggle for Indigenous Peoplehood.* Vancouver: UBC Press.

Anderson, Kim. 2000. *A Recognition of Being: Reconstructing Native Womanhood.* Toronto: Second Story Press.

–. 2011. *Life Stages and Native Women: Memory, Teachings, and Story Medicine.* Winnipeg: University of Manitoba Press.

–. 2016. *A Recognition of Being: Reconstructing Native Womanhood.* 2nd ed. Toronto: Canadian Scholars' Press.

Anishinabek News. 2008. "Anishinabek Nation Will Decide Who Are Citizens." 20 (5): 1.

–. 2018a. "Anishinabek Nation Political Update." 28 (1): 2.

–. 2018b. "We Cannot Become Extinct: Implementation of Our E-Dbendaagzijig Has to Happen Now." 28 (1): 5.

Antone, Bob. 2015. "Reconstructing Indigenous Masculine Thought." In *Indigenous Men and Masculinities: Legacies, Identities, Regeneration,* edited by Robert Alexander Innes and Kim Anderson, 21–37. Winnipeg: University of Manitoba Press.

Assembly of First Nations. 1988. *Assembly of First Nations Positions on the 1985 Indian Act Amendments or Bill C-31: A Report Presented to the Department of Indian and Northern Development Task Force by the Assembly of First Nations Chiefs Committee on Citizenship.* Ottawa: Assembly of First Nations.

–. 2011. *Virtual Roundtable on First Nation Citizenship: Highlight Summary Report.* Ottawa: Assembly of First Nations.

Baines, Beverley. 1993. "Law, Gender, Equality." In *Changing Patterns: Women in Canada,* 2nd ed., edited by Sandra Burt, Lorraine Code, and Lindsay Dorney, 243–78. Toronto: McClelland and Stewart.

–. 2006. "Equality, Comparison, Discrimination, Status." In *Making Equality Rights Real: Securing Substantive Equality under the Charter,* edited by Fay Faraday, Margaret Denike, and M. Kate Stephenson, 73–98. Toronto: Irwin Law.

Barsh, Russel Lawrence. 1993. "The Challenge of Indigenous Self-Determination." *University of Michigan Journal of Law Reform* 26 (2): 277–312.

Bastien, Elizabeth. 2008. "Matrimonial Real Property Solutions." *Canadian Woman Studies* 26 (3–4): 90–93.

Boldt, Menno, and Anthony Long. 1985. "Tribal Philosophies and the Canadian Charter of Rights and Freedoms." In *The Quest for Justice: Aboriginal Peoples and Aboriginal Rights,* edited by Menno Boldt, J. Anthony Long, and Leroy Little Bear, 165–79. Toronto: University of Toronto Press.

Borrows, John. 1994. "Contemporary Traditional Equality: The Effect of the Charter on First Nations Politics." *University of New Brunswick Law Journal* 43: 1–33.

–. 2008. *Seven Generations, Seven Teachings: Ending the Indian Act.* West Vancouver: National Centre for First Nations Governance.

–. 2010. *Canada's Indigenous Constitution.* Toronto: University of Toronto Press.

Bourgeault, Ron. 1983. "The Indian, the Métis and the Fur Trade: Class, Sexism and Racism in the Transition from 'Communism' to Capitalism." *Studies in Political Economy* 12: 50–62.

Brodribb, Somer. 1984. "The Traditional Roles of Native Women in Canada and the Impact of Colonization." *Canadian Journal of Native Studies* 4 (1): 85–103.

Brownlie, Robin Jarvis. 2006. "'A Better Citizen Than Lots of White Men': First Nations Enfranchisement, an Ontario Case Study, 1918–1940." *Canadian Historical Review* 87 (1): 29–52.

Cairns, Allan. 2000. *Citizens Plus: Aboriginal Peoples and the Canadian State*. Vancouver: UBC Press.

Calliste, Agnes, and George J. Sefa Dei, eds. 2000. *Anti-racist Feminism: Critical Race and Gender Studies*. Halifax: Fernwood Publishing.

Campbell, Maria. 1973. *Half-Breed*. Toronto: McClelland and Stewart.

Canada. 1969. *Statement of the Government of Canada on Indian Policy, 1969*. Ottawa: Queen's Printer.

–. 1970. *Report of the Royal Commission on the Status of Women in Canada*. Ottawa: Minister of Supply and Services Canada.

–. 1996. *Report of the Royal Commission on Aboriginal Peoples*. Vol. 1, *Looking Forward, Looking Back*. Ottawa: Supply and Services Canada.

Canadian Bar Association. 2010. *Bill C-3: Gender Equity in Indian Registration Act*. Canadian Bar Association, Aboriginal Law Section, Ottawa, April.

–. 2016. *Bill S-3 – Indian Act Amendments (Elimination of Sex-Based Inequities in Registration)*. Canadian Bar Association, Aboriginal Law Section, Ottawa, November.

Cannon, Martin J. 1993. "External Definitions of Self." *Nativebeat: The Beat of a Different Drum* 3 (2): 3.

–. 1995. "(De)marginalizing the Intersection of 'Race' and Gender in First Nations Politics." Master's thesis, Queen's University.

–. 1998. "The Regulation of First Nations Sexuality." *Canadian Journal of Native Studies* 18 (1): 1–18.

–. 2004. "A History of Politics and Women's Status at Six Nations of the Grand River Territory: A Study of Continuity and Social Change among the Iroquois." PhD diss., York University.

–. 2005. "Bill C-31 – An Act to Amend the Indian Act: Notes toward a Qualitative Analysis of Legislated Injustice." *Canadian Journal of Native Studies* 25 (1): 373–87.

–. 2006. "First Nations Citizenship: An Act to Amend the Indian Act (1985) and the Accommodation of Sex-Discriminatory Policy." *Canadian Review of Social Policy*, 25th anniversary ed., 56: 40–71.

–. 2007a. "Revisiting Histories of Legal Assimilation, Racialized Injustice, and the Future of Indian Status in Canada." In *Aboriginal Policy Research: Moving Forward, Making a Difference*, vol. 5, edited by Jerry P. White, Erik Anderson, Wendy Cornet, and Dan Beavon, 35–48. Toronto: Thompson Educational.

–. 2007b. "Sexism, Racism or Both? A Closer Look at the Indian Act and the McIvor Case." *New Socialist* 62: 22–23.

–. 2008. "Revisiting Histories of Gender-Based Exclusion and the New Politics of Indian Identity." Research paper for the National Centre for First Nations Governance, West Vancouver.

–. 2009. "Revisiting Histories of Racialized Injustice and the New Politics of Indian Identity, E-Dbendaagzijig (Those Who Belong)." Keynote address at a conference organized by the Anishinabek Nation, Garden River First Nation, Ontario, April.

–. 2011. "Ruminations on Red Revitalization: Exploring Complexities of Identity, Difference and Nationhood in Indigenous Education." In *Indigenous Philosophies and Critical Education: A Reader*, edited by George J. Sefa Dei, 127–41. New York: Peter Lang.

–. 2012. "Changing the Subject in Teacher Education: Centering Indigenous, Diasporic, and Settler Colonial Relations." *Cultural and Pedagogical Inquiry* 4 (2): 21–37.

–. 2014. "Race Matters: Sexism, Indigenous Sovereignty, and McIvor v. The Registrar." *Canadian Journal of Women and the Law* 26 (1): 23–50.

Cannon, Martin J., and Lina Sunseri, eds. 2011. *Racism, Colonialism, and Indigeneity in Canada: A Reader.* Don Mills, ON: Oxford University Press.

–. 2017. *Racism, Colonialism, and Indigeneity in Canada: A Reader.* 2nd ed. Don Mills, ON: Oxford University Press.

Cardinal, Harold. 1969. *The Unjust Society: The Tragedy of Canada's Indians.* Edmonton: Hurtig.

–. 1977. *The Rebirth of Canada's Indians.* Edmonton: Hurtig.

Cheda, Sherrill. 1977. "Indian Women: An Historical Example and a Contemporary View." In *Women in Canada,* edited by Marylee Stephenson, 195–208. Don Mills, ON: General Publishing.

Clatworthy, Stewart. 2003a. *Factors Contributing to Unstated Paternity.* Ottawa: Indian and Northern Affairs Canada, Strategic Research and Analysis Directorate.

–.2003b. "Impacts of the 1985 Amendments to the Indian Act on First Nations Populations." In *Aboriginal Conditions: Research as a Foundation for Public Policy,* edited by Jerry White, Paul. S. Maxim, and Dan Beavon, 63–90. Vancouver: UBC Press.

Coates, Ken. 2008. "The Indian Act and the Future of Aboriginal Governance in Canada." Research paper for the National Centre for First Nations Governance, North Vancouver.

Code, Lorraine. 2000. *Encyclopedia of Feminist Theories.* New York: Routledge.

Confederacy of Treaty Six First Nations. 2012. *Final Report on the Exploratory Process on Indian Registration, Band Membership, and Citizenship.* February 9.

Congress of Aboriginal Peoples. 2012. *Final Report: The Exploratory Process on Indian Registration, Band Membership and Citizenship.* https://www.aadnc-aandc.gc.ca/DAM/DAM-INTER-HQ-AP/STAGING/texte-text/gov_cap1_1358368127442_eng.pdf.

Coulthard, Glen S. 2007. "Subjects of Empire: Indigenous Peoples and the 'Politics of Recognition' in Canada." *Contemporary Political Theory* 6: 437–60.

–. 2008. "Beyond Recognition: Indigenous Self-Determination and Prefigurative Practice." In *Lighting the Eighth Fire: The Liberation, Resurgence, and Protection of Indigenous Nations,* edited by Leanne Simpson, 187–203. Winnipeg: Arbiter Ring.

Crenshaw, Kimberlé W. 1989. "Demarginalizing the Intersection of Race and Sex: A Black Feminist Critique of Antidiscrimination Doctrine, Feminist Theory and Antiracist Politics." *University of Chicago Legal Forum,* Article 8: 139–67.

Curry, Bill. 2007. "Appeal of Native Ruling Likely, Ottawa Says." *Globe and Mail.* June 19.

Dhamoon, Rita. 2015. "A Feminist Approach to Decolonizing Anti-racism: Rethinking Transnationalism, Intersectionality, and Settler Colonialism." *Feral Feminisms: Complicities, Connections and Struggles – Critical Transnational Feminist Analysis of Settler Colonialism* 4: 20–37.

Dhillon, Jaskiran. 2017. *Prairie Rising: Indigenous Youth, Decolonization, and the Politics of Intervention.* Toronto: University of Toronto Press.

Dick, Caroline. 2006. "The Politics of Intragroup Difference: First Nations' Women and the Sawridge Dispute." *Canadian Journal of Political Science/Revue canadienne de science politique* 39 (1): 97–116.

Doxtator, Deborah. 1996. "What Happened to the Iroquois Clans? A Study of Clans in Three Nineteenth-Century Rotinonhsyonni Communities." PhD diss., University of Western Ontario.

–. 1997. "'Godi'Nigoha': The Women's Mind and Seeing through to the Land." In Brantford Woodland Cultural Centre, *Godi 'Nigoha: The Women's Mind,* 29–41. Brantford, ON: Woodland Cultural Centre.

Eberts, Mary. 2010. "McIvor: Justice Delayed – Again." *Indigenous Law Journal* 9 (1): 15–46.

Ellinghaus, Katherine. 2006. *Taking Assimilation to Heart: Marriages of White Women and Indigenous Men in the United States and Australia, 1887–1937.* Lincoln: University of Nebraska Press.

Fanon, Frantz. 1967. *Black Skin, White Masks*. Boston: Grove Press.

Fellows, Marie Louise, and Sherene Razack. 1998. "The Race to Innocence: Confronting Hierarchical Relations among Women." *Iowa Journal of Gender, Race and Justice* 1 (2): 335–52.

Fiske, Jo-Anne, and Evelyn George. 2006. *Seeking Alternatives to Bill C-31: From Cultural Trauma to Cultural Revitalization through Customary Law*. Ottawa: Status of Women Canada.

Fleras, Augie. 2009. "'Playing the Aboriginal Card': Race or Rights?" In *The Politics of Race in Canada: Readings in Historical Perspectives, Contemporary Realities, and Future Possibilities*, edited by Maria Wallis and Augie Fleras, 75–78. Don Mills, ON: Oxford University Press.

Frideres, James S. 1983. *Native People in Canada: Contemporary Conflicts*. Scarborough: Prentice-Hall.

Furi, Meghan, and Jill Wherrett. 2003. *Indian Status and Band Membership Issues*. Ottawa: Library of Parliament, Parliamentary Research Branch.

Galloway, Gloria. 2017a. "Bennett Urges MPs to Kill Senate Amendment That Aims to Take Sexism Out of the Indian Act." *Globe and Mail*, June 8.

–. 2017b. "Feds Say They Can't Accept Senate Changes to Bill Aiming to End Indian Act Sexism." *Globe and Mail*, June 2.

Gaudry, Adam, and Chris Andersen. 2016. "*Daniels v. Canada*: Racialized Legacies, Settler Self-Indigenization and the Denial of Indigenous Peoplehood." *TOPIA: Canadian Journal of Cultural Studies* 36: 19–30.

Gehl, Lynn. 2006. "'The Queen and I': Discrimination against Women in the Indian Act Continues." In *Canadian Woman Studies: An Introductory Reader*, 2nd ed., edited by A. Medovarski and B. Cranney, 162–71. Toronto: Inanna Publications and Education.

–. 2012. "Unknown and Unstated Paternity and the Indian Act: Enough Is Enough!" *Journal of the Motherhood Initiative for Research and Community Involvement* 3 (2): 188–99.

Gilbert, Larry. 1996. *Entitlement to Indian Status and Membership Codes in Canada.* Toronto: Carswell Thompson.

Goodleaf, Donna. 1995. *Entering the War Zone: A Mohawk Perspective on Resisting Invasions.* Penticton, BC: Theytus Books.

Green, Joyce Audry. 1985. "Sexual Equality and Indian Government: An Analysis of Bill C-31 Amendments of the Indian Act." *Native Studies Review* 1 (2): 85–95.

–. 1997. "Exploring Identity and Citizenship: Aboriginal Women, Bill C-31, and the Sawridge Case." PhD diss., University of Alberta.

–. 2001. "Canaries in the Mines of Citizenship: Indian Women in Canada." *Canadian Journal of Political Science/Revue canadienne de science politique* 34 (4): 715–38.

–. 2007. *Making Space for Indigenous Feminism.* Winnipeg: Fernwood.

Greschner, Donna. 1992. "Aboriginal Women, the Constitution and Criminal Justice." *University of British Columbia Law Review* 26 (2): 337–59.

Gunn Allen, Paula. 1986. *The Sacred Hoop: Recovering the Feminine in American Indian Tradition.* Boston: Beacon Press.

Haig-Brown, Celia. 2009. "Decolonizing Diaspora: Whose Traditional Land Are We On?" *Cultural and Pedagogical Inquiry* 1 (1): 4–21.

Halberstam, Judith. 1998. *Female Masculinity.* Durham, NC: Duke University Press.

Hammersmith, Bernice. 1992. "Aboriginal Women and Self-Government." In *Nation to Nation: Aboriginal Sovereignty and the Future of Canada,* edited by D. Engelstad and J. Bird, 53–59. Toronto: Anansi.

Harris, Cheryl. 1993. "Whiteness as Property." *Harvard Law Review* 106: 1707–91.

Hauptman, Laurence M. 1988. *Formulating American Indian Policy in New York State, 1970–1986.* Albany: State University of New York Press.

Henderson, James (Sákéj) Youngblood. 2002. "Sui Generis and Treaty Citizenship." *Citizenship Studies* 6 (4): 415–40.

Henry, Frances, and Carol Tator. 2006. *The Colour of Democracy: Racism in Canadian Society.* 3rd ed. Toronto: Thomson Nelson Canada.

Hill, Janice C. Kanonhsyonni. 2014. "Where Are the Men? A Conversation with Janice C. Hill Kanonhsyonni." In *Masculindians: Conversations about Indigenous Manhood,* edited by Sam McKegney, 16–20. Winnipeg: University of Manitoba Press.

Hill, Susan M. 2017. *The Clay We Are Made Of: Haudenosaunee Land Tenure on the Grand River.* Winnipeg: University of Manitoba Press.

Hill Collins, Patricia. 2003. "Toward a New Vision: Race, Class, and Gender as Categories of Analysis and Connection." In *Privilege: A Reader,* edited by M.S. Kimmel and A.L. Ferber, 331–48. Boulder, CO: Westview Press.

Hobsbawm, Eric, and Terence Ranger, eds. 1983. *The Invention of Tradition.* Cambridge: Cambridge University Press.

Hokowithu, Brendan. 2014. "Embodied Masculinity and Sport: A Conversation with Brendan Hokowithu." In *Masculindians: Conversations about Indigenous Manhood,* edited by Sam McKegney, 98–108. Winnipeg: University of Manitoba Press.

Holmes, Joan. 1987. *Bill C-31: Equality or Disparity?* Ottawa: Canadian Advisory Council on the Status of Women.

Indian and Northern Affairs Canada. 1986. *Indian Band Membership: An Information Booklet Concerning New Indian Band Membership Laws and the Preparation of Band Membership Codes.* Ottawa: Indian and Northern Affairs.

–. 1987. *Report to Parliament: Implementation of the 1985 Changes to the Indian Act.* Ottawa: Minister of Supply and Services Canada.

–. 1990. *Correcting Historic Wrongs? Report of the Aboriginal Inquiry on the Impacts of Bill C-31.* Vol. 1, *Aboriginal Inquiry.* Ottawa: Indian and Northern Affairs Canada.

Indigenous and Northern Affairs Canada. 2013. *The Exploratory Process on Indian Registration, Band Membership and Citizenship: Highlights of Findings and Recommendations.* https://

www.aadnc-aandc.gc.ca/eng/1358354906496/1358355025
473.

–. 2017. *The Government of Canada's Response to the Descheneaux Decision.* https://www.aadnc-aandc.gc.ca/eng/14672276801
66/1467227697623.

Indigenous Bar Association. 2010. "Position Paper on Bill C-3 – Gender Equity in Indian Registration Act." Paper submitted to the Senate Committee on Human Rights, Ottawa, December 6.

–. 2017. "Bill S-3 An Act to Amend the Indian Act (Elimination of Sex-Based Inequities in Registration)." http://www.indigenousbar.ca/pdf/ibc_bill_S-3.pdf.

Isaac, Thomas. 1993. "Individual versus Collective Rights: Aboriginal People and the Significance of *Thomas v. Norris.*" *Manitoba Law Journal* 21 (3): 618–30.

–. 1994. "Case Commentary: *Corbiere v. Canada.*" *Canadian Native Law Reporter* (1): 55–60.

–. 1995. "Case Commentary: Self-Government, Indian Women and Their Rights of Reinstatement under the Indian Act, a Comment on *Sawridge Band v. Canada.*" *Canadian Native Law Reporter* 4: 1–13.

Isaac, Thomas, and Mary Sue Maloughney. 1992. "Dually Disadvantaged and Historically Forgotten? Aboriginal Women and the Inherent Right of Aboriginal Self-Government." *Manitoba Law Journal* 21 (3): 453–75.

Jacobs, Beverley. 2014. "There Has Been a War against Indigenous Women since Colonization." http://aptn.ca/news/2014/09/23/war-indigenous-women-since-colonization-former-nwac-president/.

Jamieson, Kathleen. 1978. *Indian Women and the Law in Canada: Citizens Minus.* Advisory Council on the Status of Women. Hull, QC: Government Printer.

–. 1986. "Sex Discrimination and the Indian Act." In *Arduous Journey: Canadian Indians and Decolonization,* edited by Rick J. Pointing, 112–36. Toronto: McClelland and Stewart.

Jardine, Alice, and Paul Smith, eds. 1987. *Men in Feminism.* New York: Methuen.

Johansen, B.E. 1995. "Dating the Iroquois Confederacy." *Akwesasne Notes* 1 (3–4): 62–63.

Johnson, Allan G. 1997. *The Gender Knot: Unraveling Our Patriarchal Legacy*. Philadelphia: Temple University Press.

Johnston, Charles M. 1964. *The Valley of the Six Nations: A Collection of Documents on the Indian Lands of the Grand River*. Toronto: Champlain Society, 1964.

–. 1994. "The Six Nations in the Grand River Valley, 1784–1847." In *Aboriginal Ontario: Historical Perspectives on the First Nations*, edited by Edward S. Rogers and Donald B. Smith, 167–81. Toronto: Dundurn Press.

Johnston, Darlene. 1993. "First Nations and Canadian Citizenship." In *Belonging: The Meaning and Future of Canadian Citizenship*, edited by William Kaplan, 349–67. Montreal and Kingston: McGill-Queen's University Press.

Kane, Marlyn (Osennontion), and Sylvia Maracle (Skonganleh:ra). 1989. "Our World: According to Ossennontion and Skonaganleh:ra." *Canadian Woman Studies* 10 (2–3): 7–19.

Kauanui, J. Kehaulani. 2008. *Hawaiian Blood: Colonialism and the Politics of Sovereignty and Indigeneity*. Durham, NC: Duke University Press.

–. 2017. "Indigenous Hawaiian Sexuality and the Politics of Nationalist Decolonization." In *Critically Sovereign: Indigenous Gender, Sexuality, and Feminist Studies*, edited by Joanne Barker, 45–68. Durham, NC: Duke University Press.

Khan, S., D. Hugill, and T. McCreary. 2010. "Building Unlikely Alliances: An Interview with Andrea Smith." *Upping the Anti: A Journal of Theory and Action* 10: 41–52.

Kirkness, Verna. 1987–88. "Emerging Native Women." *Canadian Journal of Women and the Law* 2: 408–15.

Krosenbrink-Gelissen, Lilianne Ernestine. 1991. *Sexual Equality as an Aboriginal Right: The Native Women's Association of Canada and the Constitutional Process on Aboriginal Matters, 1982–1987*. Saarbrucken: Verlag Breitenbach.

LaChapelle, Caroline. 1982. "Beyond Barriers: Native Women and the Women's Movement." In *Still Ain't Satisfied*, edited by

M. Fitzgerald, C. Guberman, and M. Wolfe, 257–64. Toronto: Women's Press.

Lamirande, Todd. 2019. "Women Leaders Rip Ottawa for Not Ending Indian Act Discrimination." *APTN National News,* April 9. https://aptnnews.ca/2019/04/09/women-leaders -rip-ottawa-for-not-ending-indian-act-discrimination/.

Laronde, Mary. 2007. "OTC Conference Tackles 'Indian Status' Head-On." *Anishinabek News,* May 2007, 11.

Lawrence, Bonita. 2002. "Rewriting Histories of the Land: Colonization and Indigenous Resistance in Eastern Canada." In *Race, Space, and the Law: Unmapping a White Settler Society,* edited by Sherene Razack, 21–46. Toronto: Between the Lines.

–. 2004. *"Real" Indians and Others: Mixed-Blood Urban Native Peoples and Indigenous Nationhood.* Vancouver: UBC Press.

–. 2012. *Fractured Homeland: Federal Recognition and Algonquin Identity.* Vancouver: UBC Press.

Lindberg, Tracey. 2010. "The Doctrine of Discovery in Canada." In *Discovering Indigenous Lands: The Doctrine of Discovery in the English Colonies,* edited by Robert J. Miller, Jacinta Ruru, Larissa Behrendt, and Tracey Lindberg, 89–125. Oxford: Oxford University Press.

Luk, Senwung. 2009–10. "Confounding Concepts: The Judicial Definition of the Constitutional Protection of the Aboriginal Right of Self-Government in Canada." *Ottawa Law Review* 41: 101–37.

Lyons, Scott Richard. 2010. *X-marks: Native Signatures of Assent.* Minneapolis: University of Minnesota Press.

Magnet, Joseph Eliot. 2003. "Who Are the Aboriginal People of Canada?" In *Aboriginal Rights Litigation,* edited by Joseph Eliot Magnet and Dwight A. Dorey, 23–91. Markham, ON: LexisNexis.

Magnet, Joseph Eliot, and Dwight A. Dorey, eds. 2003. *Aboriginal Rights Litigation.* Dayton, OH: LexisNexis Butterworths.

Mandel, Michael. 1989. *The Charter of Rights and Freedoms and the Legalization of Politics in Canada.* Toronto: Wall and Thompson.

Mann, Barbara Alice. 2000. *Iroquoian Women: The Gantowisas.* New York: Peter Lang Publishing.

–. ed. 2008. *Make a Beautiful Way: The Wisdom of Native American Women.* Lincoln: University of Nebraska Press.

Mann, Michelle M. 2005. *Indian Registration: Unrecognized and Unstated Paternity.* Ottawa: Status of Women Canada Research Directorate.

Manuel, Arthur, and Grand Chief Ronald Derrickson. 2017. *The Reconciliation Manifesto: Recovering the Land, Rebuilding the Economy.* Toronto: James Lorimer and Company.

Manyfingers, Morris. 1986. "Determination of Indian Band Membership: An Examination of Political Will." *Canadian Journal of Native Studies* 1: 63–75.

Maracle, Lee. 1988. *I Am Woman.* North Vancouver: Write-On Press.

–. 1993. "Racism, Sexism and Patriarchy." In *Returning the Gaze: Essays on Racism, Feminism and Politics,* edited by Himani Bannerji, 122–30. Toronto: Sister Vision Press.

Mariedaughter, Paula. 1986. "Too Butch for Straights, Too Femme for Dykes." *Lesbian Ethics* 2 (1): 96–100.

Mathur, Ashok, Johnathan Dewar, and Mike DeGagné. 2011. *Cultivating Canada: Reconciliation through the Lens of Cultural Diversity.* Ottawa: Aboriginal Healing Foundation.

Mawani, Renisa. 2009. *Colonial Proximities: Crossracial Encounters and Juridical Truths in British Columbia.* Vancouver: UBC Press.

Mccue, Harvey A. "Indian." *Canadian Encyclopedia.* https://www.thecanadianencyclopedia.ca/en/article/indian.

McIvor, Sharon Donna. 1995. "Aboriginal Self-Government: The Civil and Political Rights of Women." Master's thesis, Queen's University.

Mercredi, Ovide, and Mary Ellen Turpel. 1993. *In the Rapids: Navigating the Future of First Nations.* Toronto: Viking Press.

Miller, James Rodger. 1989. *Skyscrapers Hide the Heavens: A History of Indian-White Relations in Canada.* Toronto: University of Toronto Press.

Miller, Robert J., Jacinta Ruru, Larissa Behrendt, and Tracey Lindberg, eds. 2010. *Discovering Indigenous Lands: The Doctrine of Discovery in the English Colonies*. Oxford: Oxford University Press.

Mohawk, John. 1994. Prologue to *The White Roots of Peace*, by Paul A.W. Wallace. New York: I.J. Friedman.

Montour, Martha. 1987. "Iroquois Women's Rights with Respect to Matrimonial Property on Indian Reserves." *Canadian Native Law Reporter* 4: 1–10.

Monture, Patricia. 2006. "Standing against Canadian Law: Naming Omissions of Race, Culture, and Gender." In *Locating Law: Race/Class/Gender/Sexuality Connections*, 2nd ed., edited by Elizabeth Comack, 73–94. Halifax: Fernwood.

Monture, Patricia, and Patricia McGuire. 2009. *First Voices: An Aboriginal Women's Reader*. Toronto: Inanna Press.

Monture, Rick. 2014. *We Share Our Matters: Two Centuries of Writing and Resistance at Six Nations of the Grand River*. Winnipeg: University of Manitoba Press.

Monture-Angus, Patricia. 1995. *Thunder in My Soul: A Mohawk Woman Speaks*. Halifax: Fernwood.

–. 1999a. "Considering Colonialism and Oppression: Aboriginal Women, Justice and the 'Theory' of Decolonization." *Native Studies Review* 12 (1): 63–94.

–. 1999b. *Journeying Forward: Dreaming First Nations Independence*. Halifax: Fernwood.

Morton, F.L., ed. 1992. *Law, Politics and the Judicial Process in Canada*. Calgary: University of Calgary Press.

Moss, Wendy. 1990. "Indigenous Self-Government in Canada and Sexual Equality under the Indian Act: Resolving Conflicts between Collective and Individual Rights." *Queen's Law Journal* 15: 279–305.

Nahanee, Teressa. 1993. "Dancing with a Gorilla: Aboriginal Women, Justice and the Charter." In *Aboriginal Peoples and the Justice System: Report of the National Round Table on Aboriginal Issues*, 359–82. Ottawa: Supply and Services Canada.

National Centre for First Nations Governance. 2009. "Memorandum: Summary of the McIvor Decisions." Prepared for the NCFNG by Ratcliffe and Company LLP, June 14.

Native Women's Association of Canada. 1986. *Guide to Bill C-31: An Explanation of the 1985 Amendments to the Indian Act.* Ottawa: Native Women's Association of Canada.

–. 1992a. "Aboriginal Women and the Constitutional Debates: Continuing Discrimination." *Canadian Woman Studies* 12 (3): 14–17.

–. 1992b. *Statement on the "Canada Package."* Ottawa: Native Women's Association of Canada.

–. 2011. *NWAC Workshop on Reclaiming Our Nations Initiative: Nation-Building and Re-building – Gathering Women's Wisdom.* Community Awareness and Engagement, April–November. Ottawa: Native Women's Association of Canada.

–. 2018a. "Bill S-3: An Act to Amend the Indian Act in Response to the Superior Court of Quebec Decision in Descheneaux v. Canada." Information pamphlet. Ottawa: Native Women's Association of Canada.

–. 2018b. *Eliminating Discrimination under the Registration Provisions of the Indian Act: Culturally Appropriate Consultation with Indigenous Women – Summary Report on Consultation.* Ottawa: Native Women's Association of Canada.

Nicholas, Andrea Bear. 1994. "Colonialism and the Struggle for Liberation: The Experience of Maliseet Women." *University of New Brunswick Law Journal* 43: 223–39.

Noon, John A. 1949. *Law and Government of the Grand River Iroquois.* New York: Johnson Reprint Corporation.

North American Indian Travelling College. 1984. *Traditional Teachings.* Cornwall Island, ON: North American Indian Travelling College.

–. 1993. *Clanology: Clan Systems of the Iroquois.* Cornwall Island, ON: North American Indian Travelling College.

O'Brien, Mary. 1981. *The Politics of Reproduction.* London: Routledge.

Ottawa Journal. 1971. "Indians Attack Women's Lib." December 11.

Palmater, Pamela D. 2011. *Beyond Blood: Rethinking Indigenous Identity.* Saskatoon: Purich Publishing.

–. 2015. *Indigenous Nationhood: Empowering Grassroots Citizens.* Halifax: Fernwood Publishing.

Penelope, Julia. 1986. "Language and the Transformation of Consciousness." *Law and Inequality* 4: 379.

Perkel, Colin. 2017. "Ontario Woman Wins 32-Year Fight for Indian Status; Argued Rules Were Discriminatory." *Globe and Mail,* April 20.

Porter, Robert B. 1998. "Building a New Longhouse: The Case for Government Reform within the Six Nations of the Haudenosaunee." *Buffalo Law Review* 46 (3): 805–945.

–.1999. "The Demise of the Ongwehoweh and the Rise of the Native Americans: Redressing the Genocidal Act of Forcing American Citizenship upon Indigenous Peoples." *Harvard Black Letter Law Journal* 15: 107–83.

Ratushny, Ed. 2000. "Speaking as Judges: How Far Can They Go?" *National Journal of Constitutional Law* 11: 293–407.

Razack, Sherene H. 1999. *Looking White People in the Eye: Gender, Race, and Culture in Courtrooms and Classrooms.* Toronto: University of Toronto Press.

–. 2002. "Gendered Racial Violence and Spatialized Justice: The Murder of Pamela George." In *Race, Space and the Law: Unmapping a White Settler Society,* edited by Sherene Razack, 121–54. Toronto: Between the Lines.

Samson, Colin. 1999. "The Dispossession of the Innu and the Colonial Magic of Canadian Liberalism." *Citizenship Studies* 3 (1): 5–25.

Sanders, Douglas. 1975. "Indian Women: A Brief History of Their Roles and Rights." *McGill Law Journal* 21 (4): 656–72.

Satzewich, Vic, and Terry Wotherspoon. 1993. *First Nations: Race, Class and Gender Relations.* Scarborough: Nelson Canada.

Sawchuck, Joe. 1992. "The Metis, Non-Status Indians and the New Aboriginality: Government Influence on Native Political Alliances and Identity." In *The First Ones: Readings in Indian/ Native Studies,* edited by David R. Miller, Carl Beal, James Dempsey, and R. Wesley Heber, 140–46. Saskatchewan: Indian Federated College Press.

Schouls, Tim. 2003. *Shifting Boundaries: Aboriginal Identity, Pluralist Theory, and the Politics of Self-Government.* Vancouver: UBC Press.

Shimony, Annemarie Anrod. 1994 [1961]. *Conservatism among the Iroquois at the Six Nations Reserve.* New York: Syracuse University Press.

Silman, Janet. 1987. *Enough Is Enough: Aboriginal Women Speak Out.* Toronto: Women's Press.

Simpson, Audra. 2000. "Paths toward a Mohawk Nation: Narratives of Citizenship and Nationhood in Kahnawake." In *Political Theory and the Rights of Indigenous Peoples,* edited by Duncan Ivison, Paul Patton, and Will Sanders, 113–36. Cambridge: Cambridge University Press.

–. 2014. *Mohawk Interruptus: Political Life across the Borders of Settler States.* Durham, NC: Duke University Press.

Six Nations Lands and Resources. 2008. "Six Nations Land Claim Summaries (Basis and Allegations)." http://www.six nations.ca/LandsResources/ClaimSummaries.htm.

Small, Brenda. 1993. "The Indian Act: An External Definition of Self and Community." *Nativebeat: The Beat of a Different Drum* 2 (1): n.p.

Smith, Andrea. 2005a. *Conquest: Sexual Violence and American Indian Genocide.* Cambridge, MA: South End Press.

–. 2005b. "Native American Feminism, Sovereignty, and Social Change." *Feminist Studies* 31 (1): 116–32.

–. 2006. "Heteropatriarchy and the Three Pillars of White Supremacy." In *Incite! Women of Color Against Violence,* edited by Incite! Women of Color Against Violence, 66–73. Boston: South End Press.

–. 2012. "Indigeneity, Settler Colonialism, White Supremacy." In *Racial Formation in the Twenty-First Century,* edited by Daniel Martinez HoSang, Oneka LaBennett, and Laura Pulido, 66–93. Berkeley: University of California Press.

Stevenson, Winona. 1999. "Colonialism and First Nations Women in Canada." In *Scratching the Surface: Canadian Anti-racist Feminist Thought,* edited by Enakshi Dua and Angela Robertson, 9–80. Toronto: Women's Press.

Sunseri, Lina. 2011. *Being Again of One Mind: Oneida Women and the Struggle for Decolonization.* Vancouver: UBC Press.

Tallbear, Kim. 2013. *Native American DNA: Tribal Belonging and the False Promise of Genetic Science.* Minneapolis: University of Minnesota Press.

Tarnopolsky, Walter. 1975. *The Canadian Bill of Rights.* Toronto: McClelland and Stewart.

Tatonetti, Lisa. 2015. "'Tales of Burning Love': Female Masculinity in Contemporary Native Literature." In *Indigenous Men and Masculinities: Legacies, Identities, Regeneration,* edited by Robert Alexander Innes and Kim Anderson, 130–44. Winnipeg: University of Manitoba Press.

Thobani, Sunera. 2007. *Exalted Subjects: Studies in the Making of Race and Nation in Canada.* Toronto: University of Toronto Press.

Thomas, Jacob, and Terry Boyle. 1994. *Teachings from the Longhouse.* Toronto: Stoddard.

Tobias, John L. 1983. "Protection, Civilization, Assimilation: An Outline History of Canada's Indian Policy." In *As Long as the Sun Shines and Water Flows: A Reader in Canadian Native Studies,* edited by Ian A.L. Getty and Antoine S. Lussier, 39–55. Vancouver: UBC Press.

Trask, Haunani-Kay. 2002. "Indigenizing Human Rights." In *Dialogue of Civilizations: A New Peace Agenda for A New Millennium,* edited by Majid Tehranian and David Chappell, 213–24. London: I.B. Tauris.

–. 2003. "Restitution as a Precondition of Reconciliation: Native Hawaiians and Indigenous Human Rights." In *Should America Pay? Slavery and the Raging Debate over Reparations,* edited by Raymond A. Winbush, 32–45. New York: Amistad/Harper Collins.

Trebilcot, Joyce. 1988. "Dyke Methods or Principles for the Discovery/Creation of the Withstanding." *Hypatia* 3 (2): 1–14.

Trovat, Frank, and Laura Aylsworth. 2012. "Demography of Indigenous Peoples in Canada." *Canadian Encyclopedia.* https://www.thecanadianencyclopedia.ca/en/article/aboriginal-people-demography.

Truth and Reconciliation Commission of Canada. 2015. *Honouring the Truth, Reconciling for the Future: Summary of the Final Report of the Truth and Reconciliation Commission of*

Canada. http://trc.ca/assets/pdf/Honouring_the_Truth_ Reconciling_for_the_Future_July_23_2015.pdf.

Tully, James. 2000. "The Struggles of Indigenous Peoples for and of Freedom." In *Political Theory and the Rights of Indigenous Peoples,* edited by Duncan Ivison, Paul Patton, and Will Sanders, 36–59. Cambridge: Cambridge University Press.

Turner, Dale. 2006. *This Is Not a Peace Pipe: Towards a Critical Indigenous Philosophy.* Toronto: University of Toronto Press.

–. 2013. "On the Idea of Reconciliation in Contemporary Aboriginal Politics." In *Reconciling Canada: Critical Perspectives on the Culture of Redress,* edited by Jennifer Henderson and Pauline Wakeham, 100–14. Toronto: University of Toronto Press.

Turpel, Mary Ellen (Aki-Kwe). 1989–90. "Aboriginal Peoples and the Canadian Charter: Interpretive Monopolies, Cultural Differences." *Canadian Human Rights Yearbook* (6): 3–45.

–. 1991. "Aboriginal Peoples and the Canadian Charter of Rights and Freedoms: Contradictions and Challenges." In *The Social Basis of Law: Critical Readings in the Sociology of Law,* 2nd ed., edited by Elizabeth Comack and Stephen Brickey, 22–37. Halifax: Garamond Press.

–. 1993. "Patriarchy and Paternalism: The Legacy of the Canadian State for First Nations Women." *Canadian Journal of Women and the Law* 6: 174–92.

Van Kirk, Sylvia. 1980. *Many Tender Ties: Women in Fur Trade Society in Western Canada, 1670–1870.* Winnipeg: Watson and Dwyer.

Venne, Sharon Helen. 1981. *Indian Acts and Amendments, 1868– 1975, an Indexed Collection.* Saskatchewan: University of Saskatchewan Native Law Centre.

Vowell, Chelsea. 2016. *Indigenous Writes: A Guide to First Nations Métis and Inuit Issues in Canada.* Winnipeg: Highwater Press.

Wallace, Paul A.W. 1997 [1946]. *The White Roots of Peace.* Ohsweken, ON: Iroquois Reprints.

Weaver, Sally. 1972. *Medicine and Politics among the Grand River Iroquois: A Study of the Non-Conservatives.* Ottawa: National Museums of Canada.

–. 1974. "Judicial Preservation of Ethnic Group Boundaries: The Iroquois Case." In *Proceedings of the First Congress, Canadian Ethnology Society*, Canadian Ethnology Service, National Museum of Man Series, 48–66. Ottawa: National Museums of Canada.

–. 1981. *Making Indian Policy: The Hidden Agenda, 1968–70*. Toronto: University of Toronto Press.

–. 1983. "The Status of Indian Women." In *Two Nations, Many Cultures: Ethnic Groups in Canada*, 2nd ed., edited by Jean Elliot Leonard, 56–79. Scarborough: Prentice-Hall Canada.

–. 1993. "First Nations Women and Government Policy, 1970–92: Discrimination and Conflict." In *Changing Patterns: Women in Canada*, 2nd ed., edited by Sandra Burt, Lorraine Code, and Lindsay Dorney, 92–150. Toronto: McClelland and Stewart.

–. 1994. "The Iroquois: The Consolidation of the Grand River Reserve in the Mid-nineteenth Century, 1847–1875." In *Aboriginal Ontario: Historical Perspectives on the First Nations*, edited by Edward S. Rogers and Donald B. Smith, 182–212. Toronto: Dundurn Press.

Williams, Paul, and Curtis Nelson. 1995. "Kaswantha." Paper no. 88a, Royal Commission on Aboriginal Peoples, Ottawa.

Wolfe, Patrick. 2006. "Settler Colonialism and the Elimination of the Native." *Journal of Genocide Research* 8 (4): 387–409.

Woodward, Rocky. 1986. "Chief Wants Bill C-31 People to 'Come Home.'" *Windspeaker* 40 (4): 4.

Woolford, Andrew, Jeff Benvenuto, and Alexander Laban Hinton. 2014. *Colonial Genocide in Indigenous North America*. Durham, NC: Duke University Press.

Wright, Ronald. 1992. *Stolen Continents: The "New World" through Indian Eyes*. Penguin Books.

Index

Aboriginal peoples. *See* Indigenous peoples

An Act for the Better Protection of the Lands (1850), 31–32, 37

An Act for the Gradual Enfranchisement (1869), 32–33, 37

An Act to Amend the Indian Act (1985). *See* Bill C-31 (1985 amendment to Indian Act)

An Act to Amend the Indian Act (2016). *See* Bill S-3 (An Act to Amend the Indian Act) (2016)

An Act to Encourage the Gradual Civilization (1857), 31–32, 37

An Act to Promote Gender Equity (2010). *See* Gender Equity in Indian Registration Act (2010)

AFN (Assembly of First Nations), 88, 90–94, 98

Alfred, Gerald Taiaiake, 12, 15–16, 55, 129–30

ancestry. *See* intermarriage; matrilineal cultures; patrilineal descent

Andersen, Chris, 133*n*2

Antone, Bob, 21

assimilation: about, 55; Americanization of, 120–21; band councils, 32–33; blood quantum, 15, 71, 85–86, 96–97; early history, 31–33; genocide, as term, 134*n*6; Indian men as "persons," 31–32; logic of elimination, 16–17; off-reserve members, 82–83; patrilineal descent and property ownership, 15, 32; resistance in Six Nations, 34–35, 73–75; White Paper recommendations, 51–56. *See also* Indianness; settler colonialism; *and entries beginning with* Indian Act

authenticity, 4, 6, 55, 87. *See also* identity and belonging

band councils, elective: about, 32–33, 36, 42–43; Bill C-31 provisions, 66–67; community discord, 16, 42–43, 72; decolonization of, 20–21, 35–36;

jurisdiction, 74, 77–78; community discord, 42–43, 54–55, 68, 78; duty to consult, 113–14; either/or categories, 5–6, 19, 24, 57, 61–64; election of band councils and chiefs, 35–37, 42–43; failure to recognize, 95–97, 100, 106–7, 111, 116; hierarchy of race, status, and rights, 30–31, 33, 41–43; impact on all Indigenous peoples, 5, 17–20, 37–38, 87, 121, 131; international forums, 3, 65–66, 122–25; political climate, 53–54; power relations, 19, 42–43; racialization and sexism, 16–17, 43, 119; recent trends, 121–22; reserve system, 30–31. *See also* decolonization

interconnected racism and sexism, case law: about, 44–47, 95–98, 106–7; *Descheneaux,* 127–29; *Drybones,* 57–62; *McIvor,* 111–15. *See also* decolonization; *Lavell-Bédard, Canada v* (1974)

intermarriage: about, 39–41; as a choice with known consequences, 54, 61; divorce, 18, 30, 40, 46, 65–66; either/or categories, 5–6, 19, 24, 57, 61–64;

equality rights vs equality before the law, 59–64; Gender Equity Act, 100, 105–11, 121–22; gender inequality, 58–61; interconnected racism and sexism, 41, 58, 62–64; law enforcement by band councils, 39–40, 42; *Lovelace* appeal to UN, 3, 65–66; *McIvor,* 100–5, 107–11; Métis, 33, 133*n*2; patrilineal descent and land dispossession, 32, 49–51; political climate, 44–45, 53–54, 67–69; "woman follows man," 44, 84–87, 95–96, 126. *See also* children; interconnected racism and sexism

intermarriage of Indian man to non-Status woman: about, 18–19, 40–41, 62; band membership (after 1951), 41, 42; community discord, 40–42, 54; lack of scholarship on, 41; non-Indian, non-band member as chief, 79–80; as threat to communities, 18, 86–87; woman as Status Indian, 18–19, 40–41, 62, 115. *See also* children

intermarriage of Indian woman to non-Status man: about, 18–19, 39–40; community discord, 54–55, 68,

oral tradition: about, 7–12,
21–22, 131; creation stories, 7–10, 21; decolonization principles, 21–22;
gender roles, 7–12, 20–21;
the good life, 131; Great
Law of Peace, 8–11, 133n4;
Great Peacemaker, 9–11,
20, 21; identity and be-
longing, 6–7; Thanks-
giving Address, 8. *See also*
Indigenous peoples

patriarchy: about, 14–15, 86–
87; decolonization of, 21–
23, 131; defined, 17; early
history, 14, 28–31; heteropatriarchy, 14–16, 21–22,
45, 96; Indigenous cul-
tures, 14; interconnected
racism and sexism, 16, 40,
63–64, 86, 96; internaliza-
tion of, 16, 32, 40, 86–87;
in reserve system, 30–31;
roots in settler colonialism,
93, 95–96; "woman fol-
lows man," 84–87, 95–96,
126. *See also* patrilineal
descent; settler colonialism;
sexism
patrilineal descent: about, 14–
16, 39–40; as assimilation,
32; blood quantum, 15,
71, 85–86, 96–97; child's
contested legitimacy
(s.12(2)), 39–40, 42; to

counter land dispossession
by settlers, 49–51; double
mother rule, 103–4; father
assumed as non-Indian,
69; *Gehl*, 97–98; Indian
Act (1876, 1956), 38, 39–
40, 42; Indian Act (1985),
68–69, 101–4; *McIvor*, 101–
4; naturalization by Indian
Act, 42–43; settler colonial
model, 15–16; as threat to
matrilineal culture, 32, 40;
unknown or unstated pa-
ternity, 69, 97–98, 122,
128
Peacemaker, Great, 9–11, 20,
21. *See also* oral tradition
political organizations,
Indigenous: about, 4, 24;
citizenship issues, 105–6;
lack of resistance by, 4, 57,
95; recent trends, 106, 121;
responses to Charter rights,
24, 88–95; responses to
White Paper, 52–56
Porter, Rob, 25, 120–21,
133n4
power, Indigenous, 9–12,
19–20, 28, 130–31. *See
also entries beginning with*
Indigenous peoples
power, settler colonial: about,
19; band membership
jurisdiction, 76–78; hierarchy of race, status, and
rights, 30–31, 33, 41–43;